T0130029

WHEN REVERSE IS FORWARD

Understanding the Unusual Ways of God

STEPHEN JOHN GOUNDRY

authorHOUSE®

AuthorHouse™
1663 Liberty Drive
Bloomington, IN 47403
www.authorhouse.com
Phone: 1 (800) 839-8640

Published by AuthorHouse 05/23/2018

ISBN: 978-1-5462-3917-8 (sc)
ISBN: 978-1-5462-3916-1 (e)

Library of Congress Control Number: 2018905046

Print information available on the last page.

Scripture taken from The Holy Bible, King James Version. Public Domain

Scripture taken from the New King James Version®. Copyright © 1982 by Thomas Nelson. Used by permission. All rights reserved.

To my wife Pauline,
the love of my life

CONTENTS

CONTENTS

FOREWORD

In an age of Biblical illiteracy, it can be no surprise to discover the uncomfortable truth, that many believers don't really know God or His ways. If we ask ourselves the question: "What do we know about God outside of the Bible?" – it would be very little. While we can understand God through the prism of His creation, it is still through the Word of God - the Bible, in which our knowledge of Him is perfected. It is the Scriptures that reveal His character and His purposes and therefore no one can begin to comprehend Him without reading and understanding the Bible.

The lack of expository preaching and teaching in many churches throughout recent years has caused this major deficiency. Many Christians simply do not know the God whom they serve. They know Him sufficiently for personal salvation and for His general character but they are lacking in their knowledge of His ways. Such deficiency is a dangerous thing because the People of God in past generations have been 'destroyed for the lack of knowledge.' Their ignorance of God and His ways allowed their foolish hearts to stray and they grieved Him because they did not know Him.

This book is an effort to help rectify the general inadequacy of Biblical knowledge concerning God and His ways. By taking a look at some of the paradoxical and unusual ways of God; it is my hope that the "readers" knowledge and understanding of Him in their personal lives will increase.

As author, I have arranged the book into two parts. The first seven chapters deal with some of the paradoxical ways of

God in which the apparent "foolishness of God" is exonerated by His eventual display of wisdom.

The second half of the book with its seven last chapters deal with some of the unusual ways of God; where once again, the wisdom of God is justified in their outcome.

Matthew 11: 19 'Wisdom is justified by her children.'

1Corinthians 1: 25 'the foolishness of God is wiser than men, and the weakness of God is stronger than men.'

INTRODUCTION

In recent years, most of us have heard of someone in a leadership position say to their staff: "You've got to think outside of the box!" Those words carry the idea of promoting unconventional thoughts, so that something new or different can be conceived and then implemented. In the world of men, thinking "outside the box" can be a healthy exercise; and if the thought can be found workable, large benefits can ensue.

As for God, He doesn't have to think "outside the box" because for His imagination, there is no box! King Solomon, the wisest man to have ever lived declared that as far as the Almighty is concerned, "the heaven of heavens cannot contain Him." Indeed, our God is like a sky without limit and an ocean without depth. There are no limits to His power and abilities and yet He is not without boundaries. In relation to God's character we know from the Scriptures that He cannot lie and that what He has promised He is under willing obligation to fulfill. The Bible tells us that He has magnified His Word above His Name, which means that He is not a 'Law unto Himself.' He would never say or do something out of character because He has submitted Himself to the righteousness of His Word which is the righteousness of God Himself. What that means to us is that the God whom we serve is not a whimsical God, but rather a very trustworthy one. He declared these truths of Himself when He told His ancient people, "I am the Lord, I do not change."

So, while there is no "box" to God's power and abilities, He *has* provided a "box" in which we can understand His character and feel secure in His love; for in these personal matters "there is no variation or shadow of turning" with Him. He is forever the same.

God has, through the Scriptures, revealed His heart and mind and therefore we can know Him and His ways within the parameters of His Word. We don't have to "think outside the box" to discover who God is and what He does – we just have to "search the Scriptures." He has already given us the guidelines of His Word to lead us into all truth and to enable us to prove that what He is seen doing *is* actually *Him* at work.

The things that God has done and the things that He is now doing can all be ascertained through the "box" of His Word - the Bible. Throughout the Bible we see Him performing some amazing things which when people observed, caused them to be astounded. They marveled at what they saw and they were filled with wonder. In the ministry of the Lord Jesus Christ, they beheld things that they had never seen before! He also *said* things that they had never heard before - things kept secret from the foundation of the world! They said to each other: *"We never saw anything like this"* and *"No man ever spoke like this Man!"*

Many new and different things were done by the Lord Jesus but there was the consistency of God's nature running through them all. Not once did Jesus do something contrary to God's character. His amazing ministry was always performed within the parameters of God's character, God's nature and God's ways.

In other words, the Lord fulfilled His ministry within the "box" of God's all-sufficient will!

And so it is for us who love and serve God. We are to follow the Lord's example and do everything within the confines of God's character and within the scope of His Word. Whatever the Lord accomplishes through us will be through the Holy Spirit working in accordance with Holy Scripture.

The "box" of God's Word doesn't limit Him in His power but it does allow us to know Him; to understand Him, and to prove Him! His Word will help us corroborate His works because everything He does will be found either directly in the Scriptures or in their tenor.

As we look at the Scriptures from Genesis to Revelation we can readily see that the scope of God's sovereign power is vast. There is so much for us to explore. We can still experience head-turning miracles and providential events that leave us and the whole world stunned, and still have them remain within the context of His Word. Therefore, when it comes to living and working for God, we need to be "thinking *inside* the box" – that is the "box" of God's character and God's Word. There is a whole "world" of sanctified imagining waiting for those who will "dive" into the Biblical text and discover a very creative, expansive God, residing within.

The reader of this book will find within its pages, fourteen chapters describing some of the ways of God that exist within the "box" of His Word. This introduction is an invitation to take a look inside and see God's handiwork in the lives of His people. Some of His ways are unusual, even paradoxical; but they're all *His* ways and they're all in the *Bible*. Enjoy.

WHEN REVERSE IS FORWARD

What is reverse? Reverse is an opposite or contrary motion of direction - commonly referred to as "going backwards." Figuratively speaking, nobody likes "going backwards" because we tend to see success as always moving forwards - moving on and moving up! This is all true of course, but opposite doesn't necessarily mean opposing. "Opposing" means to act against, to resist, to hinder, to obstruct; even to combat!

So, reverse can *look* like a step in the opposite direction but can in fact provide the means for a great, forward victory - just like the classic tactical retreat that armies have performed throughout the centuries. They go into reverse in order to regroup. They can even use their reversal to lure the enemy into a trap where a surprise attack can be made upon them! One of life's anomalies is that for some things to go forward they must first be pulled back. It's like the arrow that must be pulled back in the bow before being propelled forward quickly. Most ancient siege-engines of war were built on this principle - that which will be catapulted forward must *first* be pulled back and pulled back under tension!

This dynamic is not just for old war machines - it's also for men.

Joseph was first "pulled back" in his life *before* he was launched forward to walk out of prison, meet the Pharaoh and rule all of Egypt. Moses was put into reverse gear for forty years as he tended the flock of his father in law in the desert, before God released the tension in his life and sent him to Pharaoh - with the rod of God in his hand. David didn't receive the "green light" from God to become king of Judah until he had been compelled to flee from the court of King Saul and be brought under the tensions of a fugitive. His once-successful life was sent into reverse and he could only run for his life and hide in the cave of Adullam.

All three of these men were destined to rule and all three would come to know what it's like to handle life's reversals. Yes, God knows how to make leaders!

The apostle Paul had a similar experience. Paul - then called Saul, could have been a celebrity in the Early Church because he was a famous convert to Christianity. He had gained a reputation through persecuting the Church and when he got saved, it would seem that the "stage" was set for him to maximize his new-found notoriety. Conversion had now put him into a new environment and the temptation to remain a "somebody" must have come his way.

I'm sure that the Tempter had whispered into his ear words like: "Hey, Saul! Just because you are now a believer in Jesus, it shouldn't mean that you of all people should lose your public profile. Don't you know how famous you are? Surely, this is the time to have your name out there and to get yourself heard! People are fascinated with your testimony. Just think about how many books you can sell!" But what *did* happen to Saul of Tarsus after he got saved? What *did* God do with him? What divine arrangement *did* he soon encounter?

Galatians 1:15-17

"But when it pleased God, who separated me from my mother's womb and called me through His grace, to reveal His Son in me, that I might preach Him among the Gentiles,

2

I did not immediately confer with flesh and blood, nor did I go up to Jerusalem to those who were apostles before me; but I went to Arabia and returned again to Damascus."

Upon the event of his wonderful conversion, Saul left the scene. This is a man who had known fame but had thankfully not become addicted to it. Having met Jesus in the most wonderful of ways, his only ambition was to make *Him* known. From the moment of his conversion to Christ, his singular purpose was to live for God. He sought no stage to glorify himself; neither would he allow others to put him high on a pedestal! Oh! what a disservice we do to the celebrities of our generation, who when they are converted to Christ, we immediately seek to elevate them among us; giving them our platforms and our pulpits in order that we too may share in their fame. We glory in them!

But if Paul was still here, he would tell us that *"our glorying is not good."* He would remind us that we should not glory in the "flesh" but rather respect a person for who they are in the Spirit! Can we really be surprised if those "celebrity Christians" fail to make it all the way, when all that they have known has been a continuous stream of adoration and have encountered no immediate season of personal reversal or willing obscurity in their lives?

And who is to blame for all that? All of us! We're *all* culpable if we have gloried in their flesh; in their fame, in their former success. The Church knows only One celebrity and His Name is Jesus!

This celebration of the human is clearly not God's way. He has a plan for every life and with that plan comes a personal journey for each one. The path for everyone is different and yet there are common principles of "walking with God" that encompass us all. One of those principles is that God always reduces that which He later expands! Nowhere is this more clearly seen than in the life of Gideon. Gideon was a very humble man but God was going to use him and make him famous in Israel. He was going to use Gideon to conquer in a very remarkable war but before he and his army could be elevated, they must first be reduced.

Judges 7:1-8

'Then Jerubbaal (that is Gideon) and all the people who were with him rose early and encamped beside the well of Harod, so that the camp of the Midianites was on the north side of them by the hill of Moreh in the valley. And the Lord said to Gideon, "The people who are with you are too many for Me to give the Midianites into their hands, lest Israel claim glory for itself against Me, saying 'My own hand has saved me.' Now therefore, proclaim in the hearing of the people, saying, 'Whoever is fearful and afraid, let him turn and depart at once from Mount Gilead.'" And twenty-two thousand of the people returned and ten thousand remained.'

For God to bring this victory, God must receive the glory for it!

Gideon's army was already "up against it" because his thirty-two thousand men looked pitifully inadequate to go down into the valley and fight one hundred and thirty-five thousand Midianites and their confederates. It would have been astounding if Gideon's thirty-two thousand soldiers had won the day but God was going to win the day *His* way, and so He needed to thin the ranks. The Lord knows that the heart of man is deceitful and so to preserve Israel from pride, He began to reduce them even further in their powers of ability, and He sent the major part of them home!

'But the Lord said to Gideon, 'the people are still too many; bring them down to the water, and I will test them for you there. Then it will be, that of whom I say to you, 'This one shall go with you,' the same shall go with you; and of whomever I say to you, 'This one shall not go with you,' the same shall not go.

Then the Lord said to Gideon, "By the three hundred men who lapped I will save you and deliver the Midianites into your hand. Let all the other people go, every man to his place." So the people took provisions and their trumpets in their hands. And he sent away all the rest of Israel, every man to his tent, and retained those three hundred men.'

The strategy of God was to put the army recruitment effort into reverse gear so that having lowered the pride of man in the process, Gideon would be left trusting only God for success.

The reduction of Israel's army down to three hundred men would prove to be the right amount for God to act and give Gideon the victory he was looking for.

Reversals, even for the people of God are not easy to handle but for the man and the woman who will dare to trust God, even when they have to take a step backwards, they will hear a word being whispered in their ear, saying, *'"Not by might, nor by power, but by My Spirit" says the Lord.'*

All things in the Kingdom of God are accomplished through the power of the Holy Spirit and it's obedience to Him that guarantees a successful outcome. Personal victory comes as we walk through this life with Him even though the path at times may seem to turn backwards. It's always difficult for humans to take what seems to be a retrograde step because it often strikes the "pride of life" and in a world which idolizes forward motion of all descriptions, it's hard not to feel humiliated when reversals or demotions occur.

However, there is great wisdom in taking somebody "off the stage" or "down from the ladder" because God knows that for some, they just need to be themselves for a while. A life on stage or on the proverbial ladder is a life that's constantly being measured and the eyes of people's judgment are on them and their performance all the time. Such people carry on with a smile and a positive attitude but inside they are tired and they are often looking for someone who can say to them: "You need some time-out."

This is one of the reasons why the Lord sends us into reverse gear because the "vehicle" of our lives, which incorporates our minds and bodies just simply needs the rest. Using the words of Jesus to His disciples, a preacher once said: "Come apart, and rest awhile – or come apart!" There are times then when we can be grateful to God for putting our engines into reverse thrust because then we can rest. As the Psalmist once said: *"He makes me lie down in green pastures."*

In a situation like this, God has reversed us to refresh us and to send us forward with renewed strength. Such a period of time, will on reflection, be viewed as a time when reverse had proven to have been a forward motion.

Reversing to rest is always a positive experience but there are times when the "reverse of God" is not *leaving* the "stage" but rather being asked to take a *smaller* "stage." The world calls this a reversal of fortunes. To go from a big stage to a smaller stage is more difficult than leaving the stage altogether! When you come off the stage completely you are sent into a more private world of waiting and resting; but when you are sent to a smaller stage, the reduction and the reversal of it all can really hurt. The eyes of many are upon you and they see the loss of where you are; and remember the place where you once were.

There are many pastors and Christian leaders around the

world whom the Lord has given His "gift" of the "smaller stage." They are men with great spiritual gifts and abilities who could grace the pulpits in the largest of auditoriums; but God has led them to a small church to serve the people living there. Well-intentioned people approach them and say "What are you doing here? There are so many large churches that need your ministry. Why don't you apply for a position where your life can have more influence?"

What those well-intentioned folks don't realize is that the large churches in the cities would truly be a backward step for that pastor because he has discovered that the small, backwoods church that he has been called to, is in fact the way forward for him! It may look like a retrograde step to others but to him it's the way to the "high places" in God! That small, country church is giving him "hind's feet" to walk upon the mountains of God!

Reversals in God operate like a hand-catapult in that He sends a person backwards with the objective of launching them forwards.

Being sent in what appears to be a backwards motion has to be first accepted and then handled. Victory begins when we accept the reversal as God's will. To resist Him is only to bring misery into our lives. The experience has to be handled too because it's not just a matter of going into reverse; it's also a matter of being under tension at the same time. It's one thing to wait patiently for things to turn around. It's quite another thing to wait for things to turn around while under tension!

After Jesus was baptized in the River Jordan, the heavens opened up to Him and the voice of God was heard over His life. The Holy Spirit came down upon Him in the form of a dove. It was a wonderful moment, witnessed by John the Baptist and all who were gathered there.

You talk about a "stage" being set! At that moment, Jesus

had it all, but what did the Holy Spirit do with Him? He sent Jesus into the wilderness. There were people all over Israel that needed His physical touch and to hear His wonderful words, but the apparent reversal of "time in the wilderness" was next on God's agenda. There He was, all alone in the "wilderness of testing" and under tension. He had to go without food for weeks and consequently He became very hungry.

When God sends you into reverse for testing and for proving, you must learn how to handle the tension that comes with it. It's referred to as "grace under fire." We can all be nice to people on a good day, but how nice are we when we have had a string of bad days and all of them under tension?

Thankfully, the experience of being put into reverse gear and under tension is actually working for us, because the day will come when the testing time is over, the tension is released and we are sent forward at great speed! These are the moments when opportunity and promotion arrive quickly. These are times when well-intentioned people say: "How did you get in there?" All that "pulling back" and all that tension has brought you higher up "the mountain" and the "arrow" of your life is now traveling at lightning speed! Things happen swiftly for you when the Lord sends you forward. It's like you've got your "wings" again - only this time they're much bigger!

Gideon swept through to victory in one day. Joseph was released from prison and made Governor of Egypt in one day. After the wilderness testing, Jesus returned to Galilee in the power of the Holy Spirit and news of Him went out throughout all the surrounding region. Oh, yes, when God says the work in you is done and He releases the tension, it's with great speed with which He lifts you higher! And interestingly enough, you may also find that much of your future is now predicated upon a person or an event that you encountered when you were in that time of reversal. That person and that event didn't change anything at the time, but connections were made then, that opened the "door" for you later. Being sent into reverse teaches you to trust God with the details and it teaches you to be nice to everyone! The "seeds" of your future are often hidden in the "wilderness" years.

Going in the opposite direction to what you expect can prove to be the exact place that will take you forward. It will challenge your heart and your understanding but it *will* bring success to your life.

The disciples of Jesus found this to be absolutely true when after fishing all night and catching nothing, the Lord said to them:

"Cast the net on the right side of the boat and you will find."
'*So they cast and now they were not able to draw it in because of the multitude of fish!*'

Sometimes we must suspend our understanding and our usual ways of doing things and allow the Lord to send us in the opposite direction. The opposite side of the boat was *not* where the disciples would have chosen to be, but it was the side of the boat where they *needed* to be; for in God's wisdom, even reverse can be forward!

When Second is First

It seems to be human nature to have a yearning to be the first or to be the best at something. We often see this vividly portrayed in sports when the successful player runs down the field pointing his finger in the direction of himself, reminding the crowd that he's the Number One! The drive to win the gold medal at the Olympic Games can become obsessive for some athletes, to the point where receiving a silver medal would be a disappointment for them. This desire in human nature to be the ultimate winner is admirable and scary all at the same time. When athletes compete in the spirit of sportsmanship it is inspiring, but if they have an attitude of "it's gold or nothing for me" it makes their efforts dishonorable. I've heard it said that the reason people strive to be first is because nobody remembers who came second! For many, the thought of coming second can now be found on the T-shirt that carries the slogan: *'Runner up is the first loser.'*

So, why do we want to be first? The reason why we want to be first is because first is regarded as the best! And the glory goes to the best; to the winner. There's nothing wrong with seeking to be the best at something and taking first place, for when the heart is right it's a *noble* goal to achieve. The problem is the disdain we have for "second place" - when to be seen standing *next* to the winner is seen as a personal failure! Sometimes we need reminding that silver and bronze medals are still regarded as "winner's medals."

Having said all that, being first, even in God's economy is very important. In Bible times, there was a lot of honor given to the eldest son; the one who was the "firstborn" and who opened the womb of his mother for the first time. There were particular privileges and responsibilities that came with the birth order and special blessings were given to the firstborn. As firstborn, the eldest son would inherit his father's estate and he would also receive a double portion of the assets over his brothers and sisters. When the father died, the eldest son would then assume the headship of the family, looking after his mother and all his sisters until they were married. These blessings were his birthright.

The birthright was his to keep and his to lose and sadly, there were those who lost it. The Bible tells us that Esau, the firstborn of Isaac despised his birthright. He didn't hold it in esteem and he sold it to his brother Jacob one day - for food! Reuben was the firstborn son of Jacob but he forfeited his birthright when he had sexual relations with Bilhah, his father's concubine - on his father's bed! Consequently, the blessing and the double-portion went to Joseph and by the ordination of God it bypassed his firstborn son Manasseh and came onto his second son Ephraim.

This institution of the "firstborn" has been a very serious matter and God Himself has held it sacred, affirming its validity down through the centuries. Having said that, God in His sovereign will has legally circumvented it when His purposes required it.

Cain was the firstborn son of Adam and Eve but he lost his birthright and his blessing when he murdered his brother Abel.

Genesis 4:25

'And Adam knew his wife again, and she bore a son and named him Seth, "For God has appointed another seed for me instead of Abel, whom Cain killed."

When Cain was born his mother Eve said, *"I have acquired a man from the Lord."* I have little doubt that for Eve at *that* time, her son Cain probably represented all her hopes of redemption because God had told her that in her seed, lay the Man who would deliver her and bruise the head of the serpent - that is the Devil.

She then gave birth to Abel and both boys grew into men and you know the rest of the story. At that moment, Adam and Eve were left without a "seed of promise" because Cain was now cursed and Abel was gone. He who was first was now banished from the Presence of the Lord. Where now was the biological avenue for the Savior of the World to come?

By the grace of God, Eve bore another son and she called him Seth for his name meant "appointed." That which had come first, namely Cain and Abel had gone but God appointed *another seed* for our first parents. Seth wasn't first, but he became first when Cain and Abel were taken off the scene.

Sometimes, not all the time, but sometimes - that which came first must yield to that which came second. Eve I believe, knew this truth, for although Cain was the first-born, she knew of his life and so she invested her hopes in Abel; and that's why she would have been so devastated when he was killed by his brother.

I personally think, that as a mother, she sensed that Cain was going to forfeit what he had and that Abel who was second but righteous, would have inherited the birthright. God gave her Seth to replace Abel. In the end, one way or another, that which was second became first!

The line of Seth produced the line of Shem (Noah's son) and the line of Shem produced Abraham; who through the power of the Holy Spirit produced Isaac; who later produced David; whose lineage produced Jesus of Nazareth, who is called Christ the Lord!

The whole royal line of Israel came into being because God appointed another seed for Eve. These things are the deep things of God and as such, remain His property. The Scriptures have given us insight into God's wonderful plan of redemption and the path of the Seed of Christ all the way from Seth, is now plainly seen. All these matters involve the sovereignty and foreknowledge of God. They have been His secret things throughout redemptive history and though we now understand them, we must still be careful with them because in these matters "the ground whereon we stand is holy." We are talking about the "appointments" - that is, the "ordinations" of Almighty God!

As previously mentioned, both Esau and Reuben lost their inheritance to sinful behavior, with Esau being a fornicator, among other things. He sold his birthright to his tricky brother Jacob but because he was the eldest, he was still eligible for his father's blessing. Unfortunately for Esau, he *also* had a tricky mother who conspired with her favorite son Jacob and together they deceived the old man Isaac and robbed Esau of his father's blessing!

With divine election at stake, God allowed these events to happen for the sake of His word to Rebekah when before the boys were born, He said to her *"The elder shall serve the younger."* Having allowed these events to transpire for the purposes of His election, it also has to be noted that He thoroughly dealt with Jacob over *many* years for what he had done that day. After twenty years of trials and personal difficulties, God brought him back into submission to his elder brother Esau; but the inheritance and the blessing remained with him and *his* descendants.

The lives of Esau and Reuben show us how a birthright and its blessings can be lost through sin; but because these things fall into the category of the ordinations of God, there are times when second becomes first and there's no sin involved. The classic example of this can be found in Joseph's first two sons Manasseh and Ephraim, when he brought them to his father Jacob to be blessed. At that time, Jacob was very old, and like his father before him, he too had virtually lost his sight. What happened next caused Joseph to think that his father was making a huge mistake; not being able to see properly to perform the blessing.

Genesis 48:12-20

'So Joseph brought them from beside his knees, and he bowed down with his face to the earth. And Joseph took them both, Ephraim with his right hand toward Israel's left hand, and Manasseh with his left hand toward Israel's right hand, and brought them near him.

Then Israel stretched out his right hand and laid it on Ephraim's head, who was the younger, and his left hand on Manasseh's head, guiding his hands knowingly, for Manasseh was the firstborn.

Now when Joseph saw that his father laid his right hand on the head of Ephraim, it displeased him; so he took hold of his father's hand to remove it from Ephraim's head to Manasseh's head.

And Joseph said to his father, "Not so, my father, for this one is the firstborn; put your right hand on his head."

But his father refused and said, "I know, my son, I know. He also shall become a people, and he also shall be great; but truly his younger brother shall be greater than he, and his descendants shall become a multitude of nations."

So he blessed them that day, saying, "By you Israel will bless, saying, 'May God make you as Ephraim and as Manasseh!'"

And thus he set Ephraim before Manasseh.

'And thus he set (he appointed – he ordained) Ephraim before Manasseh.'

Both these young boys stood before their grandfather that day wearing their "cloaks of innocence" - being only children at that time. So why was Ephraim, the *second* son of Joseph put before his older brother Manasseh - the firstborn son of Joseph?

There's only one word that can adequately describe what happened in that moment and it is the word "election." What is election? It is the choice of God. Election is a Divine prerogative and the purposes of God in our lives stand on *His* calling and not in *our* efforts. God has the right at any time to circumvent natural and even spiritual protocols and command that the second become the first! He is God and therefore He has the first choice.

These matters, like Joseph experienced, are sometimes difficult to understand and accept, but who amongst us is going to argue with God? Who are we to give Him advice? Shall the thing created say to Him who created it, "What are you doing?"

However, I think it can be observed that in the main, those who lose their first status have often sabotaged themselves.

Cain, Esau, Rueben - they all, as they say now, "Blew it!" And these three men are by no means alone in their self-sabotaging.

Queen Vashti, the wife of the Persian King Ahasuerus took a gamble with the king's will when she refused his command to come to the feast. Dishonoring her King and husband that day caused her to lose her royal position and consequently, she was banned from the palace. Shortly after that, young Esther was brought in to take her place.

The lesson here is this: God can appoint *another* seed.

He can always create a Seth to replace what was lost. For every King Saul whom God rejects from reigning over His people, there'll always be a David. There's always *somebody somewhere* who will fulfill *all* of God's will. For every priest like Eli and his wayward descendants, there's always a Zadok who will provide a *better* ministry and a *better* lineage for God to use. For every Judas who would steal money from the ministry and betray his Master, there's always a Matthias to take up his position and receive the honor of being one of the Twelve apostles of Jesus.

Let's put it this way: *God can always find a replacement!*

So, to those who have the privilege of being first in this life –whatever that means – I believe that the Lord would say, "Be not high-minded about it, but rather give thanks."

Being first carries privileges and responsibilities and therefore there are duties to perform for those who are in that position.

If those duties are neglected, there is always a risk of eventually being replaced by somebody else.

Paul tells us that Israel is an example of this "falling from grace." Israel was not just God's Servant; Israel was His firstborn son! When God sent Moses to speak to Pharaoh He told him to say these words: *"Thus says the Lord, Israel is My son, My firstborn. So I say to you, let My son go that he may serve Me. But if you refuse to let him go, I will kill your son, your firstborn."*

There was never a nation like Israel whom the Lord viewed as His firstborn son and there was never a nation that was given so much privilege and responsibility! They were the custodians of the promises of God, the covenants of God and the glory of God, for it was with them in cloud and in fire.

The Gentiles in that sense were second, for the salvation of God for the world was of the Jews. But now, in Christ, that is no longer the case because He has made us all into one people, giving us all access to the Father through the one Holy Spirit. This new situation has been made possible through the one perfect sacrifice for sin - the life's blood offering of Jesus Christ!

What that means in simple terms is that there are no "seconds" in Heaven. In Christ we have all been made alive and we're all a part of the church of the firstborn, Jesus Christ; who was the first to rise from the dead! The Gentiles who have come to know God through Jesus Christ might have been by nature, second; but in the heart and mind of God, they are the "elect" of God and they're just as much chosen as the Jewish people, for He chose us all in Christ before the world began! Our names were written in the "Book of Life" from the foundation of the world. Let us not be high-minded about this but rather give thanks!

In this life, there are some people who either by birth or by favor come before you; but don't get anxious about this because if God wants you in first place, He can find a legitimate way to get you there. Do you remember the story of Ruth - how she desired to be married to Boaz and come under his protective wing? Boaz was indeed a close relative of Ruth's mother-in-law Naomi, and he had a deep desire to redeem the lost estates of Naomi's dead husband and her two sons - but there was a complication.

Ruth 3:12-13

"Now it is true that I am a close relative; however, there is a relative closer than I. Stay this night, and in the morning, it shall be that if he will perform the duty of a close relative for you - good; let him do it. But if he does not want to perform the duty for you, then I will perform the duty for you, as the Lord lives!"

Long story short - Boaz was second. There was somebody closer to Naomi who had the redemption rights of the family. There was another man who had the privileges and the responsibilities of redemption and so he must be given the exclusive privilege of casting the first vote. (That's what the word prerogative means – first vote.) After some deliberations, he eventually declined the offer which allowed Boaz to come to the rescue. And so, he who was second became first - much to the delight of Ruth no doubt!

God has His ways of getting the people of His choice into pole-position. The inside lane at the front of the race is His to grant.

When the Lord is governing your life, you will always get the opportunity to meet the right person or get the right job.

If someone or if something comes your way and for whatever reason, they fail or disappoint you, try to let it go! Being human, you're possibly going to feel quite sad for a while but don't pine away over your sense of loss. There's a time to cry and there's a time to stop crying. God knows that a crushed heart needs time to heal but there can come a day when God will say to you *"Don't cry about this matter anymore."*

When the prophet Samuel was deeply saddened over the disgraceful conduct of King Saul, God said to him: *"How long are you going to cry over him. Look, I have found another; I have found a man after My own heart.")*

In 1994 I was asked to be the pastoral leader of a medical mission to Romania. It was the first mission of that kind that I ever did. There was a woman on the team that had previously been praying and looking for a Christian man to share her life with. Sometime before the mission she had met someone and she thought that she had found the one, but he broke the relationship off and wounded her heart in the process. She carried this pain quite silently throughout the mission. When we were on our final night together as a team, we were all praying together and the Lord gave me a word for her. It went something like this: *"You asked Me for bread but you think that I gave you a stone. You asked Me for a fish but you think that I gave you a serpent. I protected you in that situation."*

By that time, I was in a "prophetic flow" and there may have been more words to say; but she just burst into tears, saying that was exactly what she had said and how she had felt!

A year or so later, I met her along with her young fiancé and shortly after that they were married. He who she thought was first was not the one - but he who came second was! Ah! When second is first! When God is in it all, you will eventually discover that which was second, was always His *first* choice! It's called the mystery of His will.

WHEN LEAST IS MOST

In this third chapter on the paradoxical wisdom of God, we must now turn our attention to the principle of "when least is most." What does the word "least" mean? The definitions given to us in various Dictionaries tell us that "least" means "smallest in size, degree or importance."

What does the word "most" mean?

Again, Dictionary definitions tell us that "most" means "greatest in amount, degree or extent." These two words then are the opposite of each other. They are – as we would say to-day "poles apart." However, there lies here yet another paradox in God's Word because in the economy of God; there are some occasions when the smallest amount, the lowest of degrees and the least of importance can become the greatest in extent and effect! These are some of the ways of the "Only wise God" and if we've come to know Him through having heard His call in our lives, this subject of the "least being the most" shouldn't be unfamiliar to us. Our personal salvation runs along these very lines.

1 Corinthians 1:26-29

'For you see your calling, brethren, that not many wise according to the flesh, not many mighty, not many noble, are called.

But God has chosen the foolish things of the world to put to shame the wise, and God has chosen the weak things of the *world to put to shame the things which are mighty, and the base things of the world and the things which are despised, God has chosen, and the things which are not, to bring to nothing the things that are, that no flesh should glory in His presence.'*

This portion of Scripture is very illuminating. Here we see the deliberate choice of God in the world. The word "deliberate" comes from the root word "libra" which means weighing scales.

When something is done deliberately, it means that it has been carefully thought out, weighed in the balances of wisdom and then done on purpose. It means that the matter at hand has been carefully pondered and then accomplished. So, what that means from this portion of Scripture, is that God has - in the main, *deliberately* chosen the *least* of people from a world that is obsessed with being the *most* and with being the greatest. God has deliberated over this matter and has chosen the weak people rather than the strong. This of course makes no sense from a human point of view; for how can God influence the world if He continually bypasses capable people who are already in positions of influence? Common sense would say: "God, if You want to change the world, You've got to start choosing those who can do it the best!" Apparently, God doesn't see it that way at all. The apostle Paul reminded the Corinthians and therefore us, that even the foolishness of God is wiser than men and that the apparent weakness of God is still stronger than men.

James in his letter also echoes Paul's words when he said: *"Listen, my beloved brethren, has God not chosen the poor of this world to be rich in faith and heirs of the Kingdom which He promised to those who love Him?"*

So, this principle of "when least is most" should be familiar to us because this is how God *generally* works and this is for most of us, *our* experience with Him. Having come to know Him as our Savior, we must understand and be grateful; that God, having weighed everything in the balances of His heart, has chosen to bypass the strong and empower the weak - most of the time.

This honoring of the least is not restricted to individuals for God can also apply it to families, nations and towns! Let us now consider how the Lord can bring world-wide fame to the "least of towns."

During Old Testament times, there were some major cities in the Southern Kingdom of Judah that were large, well-built and populous in their day. The names of those cities were well-known at that time. Let's see if you know some of them: Lachish, Debir, Gerar, Hebron, Gibeon. How many of those famous places are you familiar with? Apart from Hebron, do any of those places conjure up any feelings or memories for you? All those places were great in their day but most of them have now been lost in the dust of time. Now, how does your heart and mind feel when I say "Bethlehem"? Compared to those other places, Bethlehem was a small, "nothing happening here" kind of town. But God had His eye on the place and that changed the whole equation!

Micah 5: 2

'But you, Bethlehem Ephrathah, though you are little among the thousands of Judah, yet out of you shall come forth to Me the One to be Ruler in Israel, Whose goings forth are from of old, from everlasting."

God chose Bethlehem; one of the smallest and least significant towns in Judah, to be the birthplace of the Messiah! We celebrate this small town every year all around the world. And concerning the Christmas story, the Lord's mother Mary was also a perfect choice for she too was seen as among the least. She spoke of herself when she burst into a wonderful, prophetic song, saying: *"He has regarded the lowly state of His maidservant; He has put down the mighty from their thrones and exalted the lowly."*

The same God who brought down the proud walls of Jericho is the same God who exalted little Bethlehem to universal fame.

'O little town of Bethlehem, how still we see thee lie; above thy deep and dreamless sleep the silent stars go by. Yet, in thy dark street shineth the everlasting Light; The hopes and dreams of all the years are met in thee tonight!'

"Bethlehem, you who were the least, God has made the most!"

This is God's wisdom in action! It's an amazing thing to behold!

The Jewish nation themselves are who they are today because God chose them along these very lines. He chose them on the premise that they were the least.

Deuteronomy 7: 6-8

'For you are a holy people to the Lord your God; the Lord your God has chosen you to be a people for Himself, a special treasure above all the peoples on the face of the earth.

The Lord did not set His love on you nor choose you because you were more in number than any other people, for you were the least of all peoples; but because the Lord loves you, and because He would keep His oath which He swore to your fathers....'

God chose them *when* they were small and *because* they were small. When they were the least of all peoples, God set His love upon them, blessed them, and multiplied them exceedingly. From only seventy people, God made them as numerous as the stars in the night sky and as the sand on the seashore. God's premise of deliberately choosing the "least of nations" and the "least of towns" continued throughout their history as time and again, God would choose families and individuals that no one else would.

He delighted in selecting the least of individuals whom He saw coming from the least of families.

Gideon was such a choice as that. The Lord came to him one day and declared to him that he was a "mighty man of valor." This was indeed news to him because he saw himself as unworthy of the task of taking up arms to save Israel. His response to the Lord was quite typical of one who holds themselves in such low regard.

Judges 6: 15-16

'So he said to Him, "O my Lord, how can I save Israel? Indeed my clan is the weakest in Manasseh, and I am the least in my father's house." And the Lord said to him, "Surely I will be with you, and you shall defeat the Midianites as one man."*

Gideon protested that he was the least of the least. He told the Lord that he came from the weakest clan in the tribe of Manasseh and that he was "bottom of the list" with respect to his family. When he was saying all those things to God, he didn't realize that he was fulfilling all the criteria that God was going to need to use him. The more he protested about how weak and how small he was, the more he was actually confirming his selection! He was *exactly* the kind of man that God was looking for. The Lord was about to deliver His people from their oppressors and He was going to make the "least of men" into a mighty warrior.

Gideon would soon learn this lesson all over again when

the Lord told him that his army - though small in comparison to the Midianite forces, was far too big! You know the story. His army of volunteers went down from thirty-two thousand to three hundred because the Lord had said to him:

"The people who are with you are too many for Me to give the Midianites into their hands, lest Israel claim glory for itself against Me, saying, 'My own hand has saved me!'"

Sometimes, "many are *too* many" and "much is *too* much."

There is a well-known proverb which says: "Too many cooks spoil the broth."

Let's look at another individual whom God chose on the premise that he regarded himself as the least. The first king of Israel, king Saul was chosen when he was "small in his own eyes." The Lord had sent the prophet Samuel to speak to him and when he found him, he began to reveal the things that God had in store for his life. Once again, it's interesting to observe Saul's reaction to Samuel when he hears him speak of the future that God had prepared for him.

1 Samuel 9: 21

'And Saul answered and said, "Am I not a Benjamite, of the smallest of the tribes of Israel, and my family the least of all the families of the tribe of Benjamin? Why then do you speak like this to me?"'

King Saul began his reign well, but he became a very bad king and the Lord had to remove him from the earth. However, we must always remember that when God originally chose Saul, the Bible tells us that he was a "choice young man." He was the best-looking man in the land and he was physically head and shoulders above everybody else. Furthermore, as we have noted, he was also a humble young man, coming from the smallest of the tribes of Israel with his family being the least of them. At that time then, when Saul saw himself as the least, God saw him as the most!

This now leads us quite easily to the man whom God chose to replace him. His name was David and yes, you've guessed it - he also was the least in *his* father's house! Again, God sends the prophet Samuel to go and find the man who was destined to become the next king of Israel and all Samuel is told is that God has found his man among the sons of Jesse the Bethlehemite.

1 Samuel 16: 10-13

'Thus Jesse made seven of his sons pass before Samuel. And Samuel said to Jesse, "The Lord has not chosen these."

And Samuel said to Jesse, "Are all the young men here?"

Then he said, "There remains yet the youngest, and there he is, keeping the sheep." And Samuel said to Jesse, "Send and bring him. For we will not sit down till he comes here."

So he sent and brought him in. Now he was ruddy, with bright eyes, and good-looking. And the Lord said, "Arise, anoint him; for he is the one!"'

Can you see once again, how well David fit the criteria for God's deliberate choice? In this particular matter, David was sadly inconsequential in the minds of his father and his brothers. Being the youngest in the family, he was the least of his brothers and so he wasn't even considered to be brought before Samuel. David was not only the least, he was the last - the last to stand before the prophet Samuel. But in the economy of God, many times, as we now know, the last shall be the first and the least shall be the most! And so, he who was last and least in the family became king over them all!

Not only has God chosen little towns, small nations and lowly individuals to become great, He has also chosen to use *small things* to work great miracles. Samson picked up a jaw-bone of a donkey and by the Spirit of God slew a thousand Philistines when they came to attack him. David used a sling a stone to take down a giant of a man who was like a human war-machine defying the Lord and His armies. Elijah knew that God was sending an abundance of rain when his young servant told him that he'd seen a cloud the size of a man's hand rising out of the sea.

In the ministry of Jesus, the Lord fed multitudes with just a few loaves and fishes. He taught us about the Kingdom of Heaven being like a mustard seed, which is the least of all the seeds, and yet grows greater than the herbs and becomes a tree. He also told us that when we have faith as small as a mustard seed, we can do great things, like "pulling up trees by the roots" and "moving mountains" from one place to another. The woman who had the hemorrhaging problem was completely healed after touching only the hem of His garment.

Clearly, with God, small is great; few is many and less is more! And in matters of economy, let us now visit the text which give us the classic example of when the least is the most. It's about a poor widow and two small coins.

Mark 12: 41- 44

'Now Jesus sat opposite the treasury and saw how the people put money into the treasury. And many who were rich put in much.

Then one poor widow came and threw in two mites, which make a quadrans. So He called His disciples to Himself and said to them, "Assuredly, I say to you that this poor widow has put in more than all those who have given to the treasury; for they all put in out of their abundance, but she out of her poverty put in all that she had, her whole livelihood."'

How can two mites, two tiny copper coins be worth more than silver or gold? It would seem that it all depends upon the context in which they were given. The Bible tells us here that many who were rich put in much, and for that we must praise God because there are many rich who put in nothing, or at best, a pittance. At least these rich folks were giving much! But the reason the widow gave more into the treasury was because of the personal cost to her. The rich gave out of their abundance but she gave everything she had for that day.

The Lord said to His disciples, *"Out of her poverty, she has put in all that she had; her whole livelihood."*

This poor widow gave more because the ratio of her public offering to the private sacrifice was the greatest. There are many lessons that we can learn from this moment, one of which is:

"If the rich should give out of their abundance, those who have little should *still* give out of their little." This teachable moment from Jesus tells us that we should honor the Lord whatever our income!

However, the main lesson here of course is that we cannot measure true worth with what our eyes see. When it comes to these things we must remember what God said to Samuel when he was assessing the sons of Jesse: *"Do not look at his appearance or at his physical stature, because I have refused him. For the Lord does not see as man sees; for man looks at the outward appearance, but the Lord looks at the heart."*

In all these examples of the "least" of men becoming the "greatest" of men there does seem to be a common denominator between them all and that is; at least at one time, they all had good hearts and they were all small in their own eyes. They saw themselves of lower degree and of lesser importance. They were people that the world hardly noticed, because they held nothing of this world's glory; and yet God chose to bless them and use them for *His* glory! He made the least - the most!

When Nothing is Everything

As we continue our journey of discovery through the apparent contradictions found in the wisdom of God, we must now stop and consider the paradoxical truth of "When nothing is everything."

Let me begin by saying that the life of a Christian, especially that of a Christian Minister is a very chequered one; with not only the usual "ups and downs" of life but with many diverse and even contradictory elements coming their way. The "winds of change" are many, and all the varied seasons must be patiently borne, and every effort must be made to keep Christ's Name and His ministry, blameless. Flexibility and humility are required if we are to do this well. Because we are not in control, we often find ourselves in stressful situations, but we know the peace we get from having God "in our corner" and we know the thrill that comes when God "comes through" for us time and time again! Indeed, to see the Living God show up in one's life so pointedly, makes all the difficulties encountered in serving Him fade away. The apostle Paul well-described the contrasting elements of a life that has been dedicated to God and to His service.

2 Corinthians 6: 3-10

"We give no offense in anything, that our ministry may not be blamed. But in all things we commend ourselves as Ministers of God: in much patience, in tribulations, in needs,

29

in distresses, in stripes, in imprisonments, in tumults, in labors, in sleeplessness, in fastings; by purity, by knowledge, by longsuffering, by kindness, by the Holy Spirit, by sincere love, by the word of truth, by the power of God, by the armor of righteousness on the right hand and on the left, by honor and dishonor, by evil report and good report; as deceivers, and yet true; as unknown; as dying, and behold we live; as chastened, and yet not killed; as sorrowful, yet always rejoicing; as poor, yet making many rich; as having nothing, and yet possessing all things."

What Paul is saying to us here is that in the Christian life, we must expect many alterations to our circumstances and be able to handle adverse conditions. We have to walk through a world of opposites! We can be sorrowful yet rejoicing. We can be poor and yet make many rich. We can be unknown and yet well-known. We can be viewed as deceivers and yet be true. We can be regarded by some with honor and by others, dishonor. We can have nothing and yet in God, possess everything!

In other words, the Christian has to have a completely different mind-set compared to the world. This world makes every effort to avoid these contradictory elements becoming their reality; and that's why people are so desperate to climb the proverbial "ladder of success" - which pledges an upwardly mobile trajectory of one's life without interruption. For people in this world, there's only one thing better than success and that's *continued* success! They don't want to think about life's changing nature and its inconvenient variables, so they aim for the top, where "money answers everything." And this "music" never stops! The "drum-beat" goes on well beyond people's working lives as the television commercials inform retirees how they can take out a "reverse mortgage" or how they can continue to reinvest their funds. Even those who are still in their working lives are now being asked: "How long will your retirement funds last?" People's lives are spent pursuing money so that they can "flat-line" all the peaks and troughs of life and live comfortably for the rest of their lives.

The cemeteries are full of rich, dead, people!

I don't want to die having a lot of personal wealth. Obviously, I want to fulfill my duties to my wife, my children, and my grandchildren, for the Book of Proverbs says, *"A good man leaves an inheritance to his children's children."* After that, the less I have in the bank at the end of my days - the better.

John Wesley, the father of Methodism gave vast sums of money to the poor all through his life, and when he died in 1791, the only money mentioned in his will was the miscellaneous coins which were found in his pockets and in his dresser drawers. All his life, John Wesley's teaching on money provided practical guidelines for every believer. Apparently, he had only three rules about money: "Gain all you can, save all you can and give all you can!" Like Wesley, we all came into this world with nothing and it is certain that we will leave this world with nothing, but for the Christian who has had his life redeemed, he may leave *this* life with nothing but he will inherit *everything* in the next! I don't know about you, but I don't want to go to Heaven having been a hoarder down here.

If you follow Jesus, He will teach you how to provide for yourself and your family and even for the needs of others; but He'll never lead you down the path of hoarding your treasures, because from Heaven's perspective hoarding is a complete "waste of money."

If you follow Jesus, He will teach you how to believe in Him for your provision - how to trust Him for your "daily bread." He will introduce you to His Father and you too will come to know Jehovah Jireh - the "God who provides."

This chapter regarding the paradoxical truth of "having nothing yet possessing all things" is about the provision of God in your life when circumstances change; when living conditions are altered; when you find yourself in need; and when like the apostle Paul said, "you feel like you are dying, and yet, you live!"

As has already been noted, if there's one thing we all fear in this life, it's to be left with nothing. We will do everything we can to stop that from happening. But sometimes, "nothing" is required. Before God can release His "everything," we must first know His "nothing." The Scriptures have many examples of this principle at work.

Genesis 22: 1-2

'Now it came to pass after these things that God tested Abraham, and said to him, "Abraham!" And he said, "Here I am."

Then He said, "Take now your son, your only son Isaac, whom you love, and go to the land of Moriah, and offer him there as a burnt offering on one of the mountains of which I shall tell you."

Here is an example of a man being reduced to nothing in order to possess everything. Abraham had previously been in this position when he had no son and heir from his wife Sarah. Old age had come upon them both and as far as the prospect of having natural descendants, it simply couldn't exist because pregnancy for Sarah had become an impossible dream. Abraham came to know the "nothing" experience of God. But then God gave him everything he'd ever wanted and fulfilled His promise to him by giving him a son through Sarah in his old age. He had the pleasure of seeing the lad grow up before him. All of Abraham's hopes were in that boy but

God brought Abraham into a situation in which the thing that he had been given and had held so dear would now be required of him - because *all* things are God's!

(That's a statement worth repeating - all things are God's. If we remember that fact, it will help us to hold lightly to everything we have.)

Abraham was faithful to God's request and he was willing to be left with nothing. When he laid Isaac on the altar and was about to bring the knife down, the Lord spoke to him from Heaven saying: *"Abraham! Do not lay your hand on the lad or do anything to him; for now I know that you fear God, since you have not withheld your only son, your only son, from Me."*

God was effectively saying to Abraham: "Since, for the sake of My will, you have been willing to go down to nothing and have been prepared to have no line of descendants after you, I will now bless you." I will multiply your descendants as the stars of heaven and as the sand of the sea-shore. In your seed, all the nations of the earth shall be blessed, because you have obeyed My voice."

In the very moment when Abraham thought he was going to be left with nothing, God stepped in and gave him everything! In the crisis moment of Abraham's life, God intervened and gave him his son and his future back in a very big way. In that instant, God gave him the offering for the sacrifice; providing a ram instead of Isaac, which had been caught by its horns in the nearby bushes. And it can also be said that God was revealing that day what He Himself as a Father of an only Son would do in that very place many years later. Jehovah Jireh - the "God who provides" would be seen once more on Moriah's hill. God's very own Son; His very own "everything" would for a moment in time, leave God Himself with the feeling of "nothing" - until three days later when the Son, the risen Son, would become the Father's "everything." Just as Abraham gave all that he had to Isaac, so God the Father has given all things to His Son, Jesus! The Son of God is the Father's world! He has committed all judgment and all authority to Him and has caused all the fulness of God to dwell in Him!

What we learn from these examples is that it's not just about having nothing; it's about having nothing before *God*! When God is in the equation, nothing becomes the pre-requisite for His provision and supply! It's only in God that a person can have nothing and yet possess all things.

Elijah, having brought the judgment of drought and famine upon Israel by causing the heavens to withhold their dew and rain, had to hide for his life. At that time, he was alone and all that he had were the clothes that he wore. He who had brought proud Israel to its knees was sent by the Lord to hide at a remote location and there by a brook he was reduced to nothing. He had no shelter, no friends and no food! But God had Elijah's "nothing" experience turned into a "possessing all things" experience when He sent ravens twice a day to feed him with bread and meat. Elijah found Jehovah Jireh - the "God who provides" at that quiet, lonely, brook.

What is it that we all fear? We fear having nothing. We fear the possibility of running out of supply. In the realm of the human, these are rational thoughts but in the economy of faith, the fear of having nothing is irrational because God will not and can not ever leave us!

After the brook dried up, God sent Elijah to another place where there was a widow who was down to her last meal. The famine had been so severe that she and her son were just about to enter into their "nothing left situation." It looked like it was all going to be over for them very soon, but what she didn't realize is that God had just stepped into the situation! At that very moment, she was challenged to honor God by willingly serving Elijah first and deliberately going *into* nothing. You see, it's one thing to *end up* with nothing and another thing to willingly go *into* nothing! The world is not kind to those who end up with nothing, but for those who follow God *into* nothing, they find a door-way into God's inexhaustible supply! The widow took a step of faith and made a small cake first for Elijah and then for herself and her son. Having sown a seed into the kingdom of God she then discovers that her bin of flour and her jar of oil have just become gifts that keep on giving! The flour in the bin and the oil in the jar did not diminish until the drought was over!

Oh, how we hate to be in need, but Oh, how God relishes those moments in our lives, because if we're faithful in those times, He can not only add to what we have, He can multiply it too! With God, an invitation *into* nothing is a future promise of receiving everything! We all have to trust in the Scripture which says, *'Faithful is He who promised.'* If God ever leads you into an experience like this, please resist the temptations to try and fix the problem yourself. If you put your own hand to it and endeavor to make the problem go away, you may get yourself out of "Dodge" but you will probably find that there's another "Dodge City" experience waiting for you. The temptation to put your own hand into the equation in order to avoid being reduced to nothing is very strong and it was one of the temptations that came to Jesus when He was tested in the wilderness.

St. Luke 4:1- 4

'Then Jesus being filled with the Holy Spirit, returned from the Jordan and was led by the Spirit into the wilderness, being tempted by the devil. And in those days He ate nothing, and afterward, when they had ended, He was hungry.

And the devil said to Him, "If you are the Son of God,

command this stone to become bread." But Jesus answered him saying, "It is written, 'Man shall not live by bread alone, but by every word of God.'"

There was Jesus, alone in the wilderness, and with nothing to eat. All of this situation was God's will for Him at that time because He was led by the Holy Spirit *into* that predicament. Jesus was *led into* His "nothing" experience! There are some predicaments that are man-made and some which are God-made. This one was God-made. That means that as bad as this situation was and as tough as His conditions were, God was in the equation! Everything in this scenario was engineered by God. All the dangers of the wild beasts; the brutal temperatures; and most importantly, the amount of time spent the Lord spent there. The difficulties Jesus encountered were all calculated to make Him very weak and very hungry. God brought His Son into a "nothing situation." No water, no food, no friends, no comforts. Then when He was at the height of disadvantage, the devil himself came to Him and what did he do? Did he tempt to Him to do something really bad? No. The devil just suggested something to Him.

What did he suggest? He suggested that if He was indeed the Son of God, that He should use His powers to fix His problem. *"If You are the Son of God, command that this stone to become bread."* "You of all people shouldn't be left in a "nothing situation" like this! You gotta eat!"

The devil tempted Jesus to cancel out the *"nothing"* that God had *given* Him! But Jesus, as a man born of a woman and made under the Law of God, responded accordingly saying: *"It is written that man shall not live by bread alone, but by every word of God."* It wasn't long after that moment that the devil left Him and God sent some of His angels to minister to

Him. (It wouldn't surprise me to learn that the angels brought Him His favorite food.)

What is of great importance here is that while Jesus went into the wilderness to experience the trials that test a man, He returned to Galilee in the *power* of the Holy Spirit. He'd gone into the wilderness to taste the "nothing" of God's providential arrangement but He came out of that desert with God's "everything." He came out stronger and with the power of the Holy Spirit upon Him. The Spirit of God was on Him without measure! God had used the wilderness to prove His obedience and turn His "having nothing - yet possessing all things" into reality when angels were sent to minister to Him. When Jehovah Jireh is your God, there are no situations beyond His ability to provide for you!

Miracles of God's provision can happen at any time but I think that they are most likely to come when the need is the highest. How often do we say: *"That person needs a miracle!"* What are we saying when we say that? We're saying that the situation has become so dire that only a miracle can change it.

There were two sisters whom Jesus loved and they had a brother who was very ill. The sisters sent messages to Jesus informing Him of the situation and hoped that He would come in time to heal him. The sisters feared losing their brother and of being left with no hope of recovery. They were fighting the prospect of death and of having a "nothing experience."

Jesus knew it and He also knew that "something" is still not "nothing" and to fulfill God's will in this situation, He must wait until the sisters' "something" had become their "nothing."

'Martha said to Jesus: "Lord, if you had been here, my brother would not have died." Martha was effectively saying to Jesus that if He had come earlier they would have had "something" to hold on to. What the sisters didn't understand

is that on this occasion, God needed their "something" to fade to "nothing" so that out of "nothing" God could give them back "everything" they desired!

When it comes to God and His provision, let us not be too quickly afraid of having "nothing" because after the crisis is passed, God can give you His "everything" and He can do it all in one day if He has to! Believe me, He has the ability to really surprise you!

So, let us be faithful through our times of "nothing" and put our trust in Him who can not only abundantly supply from little but who can even raise the dead from nothing!

God knows what He's doing. Isaac was always going to be Abraham's everything, even if God had to raise him from the dead! This then is another facet of the paradoxical ways of God in our lives. Let us accept it as a manifestation of His wisdom and let us join the ranks of those who've walked this path. May we be counted among those who have known God as Jehovah Jireh, having at times nothing, yet possessing everything.

WHEN LITTLE IS BIG

There are many things in life that everyone can easily take for granted and the main reason is that we have a tendency to ignore little things - whatever they are and whoever they are.

For example, we can all appreciate a solid oak door but the little hinges upon which that very door swings are completely over looked; and yet what is a big door *without* little hinges? Here in this chapter lies another "spiritual coin" with two sides for you to consider: "When little is big." What is meant by that is: what is small and seemingly insignificant can have a major part to play today and have a huge outcome later. The "key" to unlock our understanding in this matter comes from our ability to see potential whether good or bad.

Sometimes, we only see the things that are right in front of us and we miss all the smaller details. Most of us are so consumed with the "production" on center-stage that we are unaware of all the surrounding and contributing factors that are making the "show" a success.

It seems that we all have the propensity to allow small things to go unnoticed and unappreciated and the reason why we do it is because we fail to see their function and their potential. In this life then, little things are easily overlooked or disregarded. God is well-acquainted with this part of human nature and that's why in the past, He's asked even His own people the searching question: *"Who has despised the day of small things?"*

God teaches His people everywhere to view every little thing in light of its function, its future and its potential. As the proverbial saying goes: *"Mighty oaks from little acorns grow."*

I think that if we're honest with ourselves, we've all "passed by on the other side" and ignored something or someone small.

We've regarded it as insignificant because it couldn't do anything for us that day. Its only "voice" had been a quiet one and we didn't have the "ears" to hear it. We didn't discern the God-given "seed of potential" and so when we heard the little child say: "When I grow up, I'm going to be...." it just came across as cute and we failed to see their future greatness and kingdom impact!

The truth is that nothing that God is involved in can be glibly dismissed or viewed as trivial. The very opposite of that is true and there are rewards attached to *everything* done for Him.

Matthew 10: 41- 42

"He who receives a prophet in the name of a prophet shall receive a prophet's reward. And he who receives a righteous man in the name of a righteous man shall receive a righteous man's reward. And whoever gives one of these little ones only a cup of cold water in the name of a disciple, assuredly, I say to you, he shall by no means lose his reward."

In these verses we see the Lord revealing different levels of service and reward. Beginning with the "prophet's reward" he then goes on to speak of a "righteous man's reward" and then He talks of a reward for the one who gives only a cup of cold water to a child in the name of a disciple! A little cup of cold water given to a child does not go unnoticed by God and is not without significance in His heart and mind. An act like that is regarded in Heaven as having done a "little big thing" and

40

it goes down in the record books of Heaven. *"Suffer the little children to come unto Me and forbid them not, for of such is the kingdom of Heaven"* Jesus said.

All children are God's little, big people! They are the angel's delight and their special wards of care.

Not only are children God's delight, they are also His special instruments upon which He plays significant "tunes" in adult lives.

The Scriptures give us some examples of how the Lord uses young people to affect life-changing moments in "the great and the good." I'd like to take a look at two examples of good yet proud men who experienced God working in them, using the *seemingly* insignificance of a young girl. The men were very dissimilar in character and their experiences in life were very different; but both of them in one way or another, came under the humbling power of what the King James Bible described as the "little maid."

Let us now consider the first man. His name was Naaman. He was a Syrian and he was a great man in his nation. He was honorable, brave and proud.

2 Kings 5: 1-14

'Now Naaman, commander of the army of the king of Syria, was a great and honorable man in the eyes of his master, because by him the Lord had given victory to Syria. He was also a mighty man of valor, but a leper. And the Syrians had gone out on raids, and had brought back captive a young girl from the land of Israel. She waited on Naaman's wife.

Then she said to her mistress, "If only my master were with the prophet who is in Samaria! For he would heal him of his leprosy." And Naaman went in and told his master, saying, "Thus and thus said the girl who is from the land of Israel."'

Here is a great man, living not only rich, but high. He was a favorite of the king of Syria and highly esteemed in his country for the military victories that he had accomplished - even over Israel at times! Now it was the Lord who had enabled him to do these things, but he, as they say, knew it not! Naaman had everything this life could offer. He had both riches and honor and yet there was a huge drawback to his life. He was a leper! He was smitten by that horrendous disease of the flesh.

Naaman's life serves as a reminder to us all, that no one's wealth or honor can take them out of the reach of personal calamity. Naaman was as great as this world could make him and yet there wouldn't have been one slave in Syria that would have traded places with him! (Those that have wealth, yet need health, will all tell you what they value the most!)

For Naaman, his leprosy was like a dark cloud on a clear day.

But as God's loving Providence would have it, there was an "open door" to his healing and it resided in his *own* house - if he could just see it! There was someone in his own house who held the key that would unlock the door to his deepest problem. There was someone actually living with him who could be the "hinge" on which the "great door" of his situation could swing wide open.

In front of him, there is a young, captive Israelite who has been living in his house, serving his wife *every* day. She had previously been taken prisoner from one of the many raids that the Syrians had made into Israel. She served Naaman's wife and she was close enough to know how distraught they both were about his disease. One day, she told her mistress about the prophet of the Lord who lived in Samaria, and how that if her master Naaman could only be with him, that he would heal him.

Naaman was a proud man, and proud men usually have "small ears" but when desperation kicks in, the ears tend to be more open and upon hearing his wife's account, he decided that he had nothing to lose. He went to *his* master the king of Syria and told him the whole story and so the king of Syria sent him to the king of Israel with an official letter, saying: *"I have sent Naaman my servant to you, that you may heal him of his leprosy."* When the king of Israel read the letter, he panicked and took it all the wrong way. Elisha, the prophet heard about it and he told the king to let Naaman come to his house. So, Naaman in his chariot and horses along with his soldier-servants presented himself at Elisha's door.

Being the military planner that he was, he had it *all* worked out in his head. His pride conjured up a scenario that would take into consideration his status. He had the *whole* ceremony of healing mapped out in his mind - just ready to press "play." And that's what proud, powerful, dominant people do when they have to bow the knee and humble themselves - they continue to hang on to their pride for as long as they can. Nothing of what he imagined actually took place! Nothing! Nothing except the outcome!

First, the prophet didn't even come to the door to meet him but sent a messenger with the "word of the Lord" which was this: *"Go and wash in the Jordan river seven times and your flesh shall be restored to you and you shall be clean."*

Naaman was furious and began to leave in the heat of his spirit, mumbling to himself about it all. This was *not* the plan that he had in his head because he wanted to be cured *his* way - with his dignity intact. He went away in a rage, the Bible says.

Behold the folly of pride! His knee-jerk reaction to it all was about to rob him of his miracle and it would have been completely his own doing. However, his servants knowing that he was indeed a good man; they spoke to him with respect, calling him "father" and they managed to make him think again.

"If the prophet had told you to do something great, something difficult, would you not have done it? All you have to do is wash and be clean."

Upon hearing that advice, and with nothing to lose but a bit of pride, Naaman had second thoughts and he relented.

'So, he went down and dipped seven times in the Jordan, according to the saying of the man of God; and his flesh was restored like the flesh of a little child, and he was clean.'

By listening to the *words* of a child, Naaman received the *skin* of a child! Oh, how the events of that day could have been so different had he not listened!

Proud men and women are their own worst enemies, and it's so easy for them to miss God! It's easy for them to overlook people and not even see that the answers to their greatest problems can sometimes be right under their noses. They don't seem to be able to see the things that are hidden in plain sight!

This miracle of God in Naaman's life began with the faith and the words of a little maid. The young slave girl living in his house was the key to unlock the door to his healing and solve his dilemma. I'm sure that upon returning home, Naaman rewarded her for what she had said and furthermore, I'm sure that God did much of this *just* for *her*. She may have been a girl without her country but she was *not* without her God!

Now, let's consider the example of the second man. His name was Peter - Simon Peter. He was one of the chief disciples of the Lord. He was a good man and full of good intentions, but the pride of life was wrapped around his heart and soul. He too would encounter God's "little maid" but in a way that he could never have expected!

Mark 14: 27- 31

'Then Jesus said to them, "All of you will stumble because of Me this night, for it is written: 'I will strike the Shepherd, and the sheep will be scattered.' But after I have been raised, I will go before you to Galilee."

Peter said to Him, "Even if all are made to stumble, yet I will not be." Jesus said, Assuredly, I say to you that today, even this night, before the rooster crows twice, you will deny Me three times."

But he spoke more vehemently, "If I have to die with You, I will not deny You!" And they all said likewise.'

It was a shocking statement that Jesus made when He effectively said to His disciples, *"All of you will be offended/ stumble/fall because of Me this night."* They *all* agreed with each other when they said they would rather die than deny knowing Him, but it was Simon Peter that led that whole conversation. *"Even if everyone is made to fall tonight, I won't!"* he said.

"I will go to prison and even death with You" he went on to say. Jesus told him that he would deny him three times, but again he said, *"If I have to die with you I will not deny You!"*

Peter was speaking in the emotion of the moment and in the spirit of pride.

"These guys might deny You – but not me! *You* can count on *me*! I have "got your back" Lord!" At that moment, Simon Peter was telling Jesus that both He and the Scriptures were incorrect! The very Scriptures of Truth which cannot fail or be broken were now being contradicted because Simon Peter thought that he knew better. His pride would not let him see that when the Scriptures had recorded that *all* the sheep would be scattered, that it included *him*! *Behold the folly of pride!*

Mark 14: 66-72

'Now as Peter was below in the courtyard, one of the servant girls of the high priest came. And when she saw Peter warming himself, she looked at him and said, "You also were with Jesus of Nazareth." But he denied it, saying, "I neither know nor understand what you are saying." And he went out on the porch, and a rooster crowed.

And the servant girl saw him again, and began to say to those who stood by, "This is one of them." But he denied it again. And a little later those who stood by said to Peter again, "Surely you are one of them; for you are a Galilean, and your speech shows it."

Then he began to curse and swear, "I do not know this Man of whom you speak!"

A second time the rooster crowed. Then Peter called to mind the word that Jesus had said to him. "Before the rooster crows twice you will deny Me three times." And when he thought about it, he wept.'

There's not much that we can add to the account of this sad event. In a sense, we can all feel his pain. A rooster crowed at the first denial but it seemed that he didn't get the message. By the time the rooster crowed again, he had denied the Lord three times and *then*, Peter called to mind the word that Jesus had said to him. (Before we condemn Peter too quickly, we must ask ourselves: "Do *we* always regard the signs that God is giving us or is it our experience that we only "get it" when the "rooster" has crowed twice - when it's too late and the damage has been done"?)

Peter would soon have to leave the scene and be "scattered like all the other sheep" just as the Scriptures had foretold. Devastated, he would eventually go into hiding and cry his soul out! It was the worst moment of his life because that night, he had met God's "little maid" and he stumbled and fell like a great tree being cut down in the forest. The "axe" was laid to the "root of the tree" and his whole personality unraveled in slow-motion.

The "little maid" said to him as he warmed himself by the fire: *"You also were with Jesus of Nazareth."* *"I don't know what you're talking about"* he replied. He left the courtyard and went to the porch and there she was again. And she said to those who were there, *"This is one of them."* Again, Peter denied everything. A few moments later, those around him said to him, *"Surely, you are one of them; for you are a Galilean and your accent shows it."* *"I do not know this Man of whom you speak!"*

And the rooster crowed! Oh, that third denial brought it all right out of his mouth! I think that this is the sentence that haunted him and caused him to "cry a river." Its words must have constantly played and re-played in his mind - *"I do not know this Man of whom you speak!"*

His sin was huge, for to deny the Lord before men is an eternal issue and anyone doing that will have the Lord denying *them* on Judgment Day. He will *not* confess *their* names before His Father and the holy angels.

Thankfully, there was a "gift of repentance" given to Simon Peter but it was a bit "touch and go" for a moment - it wasn't a simple, foregone conclusion. That very night, as Jesus was talking to them all about what was to happen, He said: *"Simon, Simon! Indeed, Satan has asked for you so that he may sift you like wheat!"* Whom did Satan ask to have Simon Peter? He asked the ultimate authority. He asked God for him. The life of Simon Peter was well known to Satan and on occasions, had found easy access into his soul. Yes, Satan would have *this* man, for his pride was strong and his sin was great. Mercifully, Peter had an advocate in Jesus and so the Lord Himself interceded for him and pleaded with God for him. Jesus effectively said to him: *"Satan wants you Simon, but I have prayed for you! I have prayed to God that your faith shouldn't fail and that after you have returned to Me in your heart, you must strengthen your brothers."*

Jesus revealed *all* of this before the events of that night took place, but when Jesus spoke these words, they fell on deaf ears. They were spoken to a man wrapped up in the pride of life. *"I am ready to go with You both to prison and to death!"* he protested. That night, Simon Peter would be brought to his knees. Waiting for him on that fateful evening was a young girl - one of God's "little things" - and down he went! *"Oh, how the mighty have fallen!'* Simon Peter fell down at the words of the young servant girl and his life became "unhinged."

Two very different men; Naaman and Simon Peter. Two very different scenarios. But what do they have in common? Both men were caught in the pride of life and both men were humbled by one of God's "little big things." For Naaman, the "little maid" was God's small instrument to bring healing into his life if he could humble himself to act on her words. For Simon Peter, the "little maid" was God's small "weapon of choice" to break his foolish pride once and for all.

God's "little maid" will probably show up in *our* lives at some time or another. If we're too high in our own estimation, we will undoubtedly miss her and consequently miss our miracle from God. And if we become proud, even in our service for God; then God will have a "little maid" waiting for us one day, and out of the innocence and sincerity of her heart, she will speak the truth - and it will be devastating! She is the Lord's instrument of blessing *and* of judgment - *a little, big thing!* This paradoxical principle instructs us to honor everyone, for it teaches the "big head" to value the "little toe." This contrasting truth of "When little is big" is a reminder to us all to view everyone and everything as God does, and not to dismiss them as of no real consequence.

One day in the life of Jesus, the disciples of the Lord found themselves in a major situation; when surrounded by multitudes of people, He asked them the question: *"Where shall we buy bread, that these may eat?"*

Philip answered Jesus: *"Two hundred denarii worth of bread is not sufficient for them, that every one of them may have a little."*

Andrew said: *"There is a lad here who has five barley loaves and two small fish, but what are they among so many?"*

The solution to the problem was found in a little boy and what he had to offer. This young boy could have so easily been dismissed but the Lord who sees and cares about everyone and everything saw his potential and a miracle of provision ensued.

We all must resist the temptation to dismiss the little things because they all have the power to "make or break" us. Didn't James tell us about the dangers of the tongue; how that such a little member can boast of great things? He described the tongue as a "fire" which can burn a whole "forest" down!

None of us can afford to ignore the apparent small things in life if they have the potential to ruin us! How many bankrupt millionaires and once-rich celebrities have confessed that somewhere along the way, they lost the value of a dollar? Along the way, their personal values subtly changed and before they knew it, they had lost their former selves and allowed their wealth to transform them into someone else! Over time, they had become big in their own eyes and money had lost its true value. (A hundred dollars to a rich man is a tip he may give to his chauffer, but to an orphanage in Romania, a hundred dollars is food for the week, for everyone!)

Children are God's jewels. They are His "little big things."

Isn't a diamond a little, big thing? Haven't we all heard it said: "Did you see the size of that "rock" that he put on her finger?" When a small engagement ring becomes the only thing in the room that people are looking at; that is "when little is big."

WHEN FAILURE IS SUCCESS

Throughout the Scriptures we read of both people and things failing. Some of those failures seemed final, but their "death" brought in a new dynamic and some failures just proved to be "bitter lessons" learned. Either way, success was drawn out of both. This is yet another paradoxical principle in the wisdom of God - "When failure is success."

The reason why failure carries such dread is because of the sense of finality that it produces in us. None of us want to be left without a "chair" when the "music" stops and we will do everything we can to avoid such a moment. It comes therefore as a surprise for many when they discover that God often seeks out such scenarios. The dead-end that *we* dread is *His* moment to introduce a new thing that will initiate *His* success.

When Hagar, the wife of Abraham, had to leave with her son Ishmael, she was given bread and a skin of water for her journey. She wandered in the wilderness with her son, and as a result, all the water in the skin was used up. It seemed like the "end of the road" for her and her son, and all she could do was shelter the boy under some shrubs and then cry. At that point, her whole life felt like a failure but the "God Who Sees" came to her rescue and opened her eyes to that which she previously could not see, and she saw a well of water. She went and filled the skin with water and gave her son a drink. What this story shows us is that revelation and new provision can come after apparent failure. From that moment on, Hagar's provision was not from the bottle nor from Abraham but from the "God of the water-bottle" and the "God of Abraham." She just had to be brought to the end of herself to find Him.

It comes as a revelation to our hearts that God sometimes needs failure to arrive in order for a fresh start to begin. That's why He allows things to wind down over time because He has a new day in view; but He can't bring in the new until the old has gone.

When God raised up Joseph to rule Egypt, He didn't just have the "feeding of the world" in mind; He had the *long-term* blessings of His people to consider. To accomplish this, He must bring Egypt to experience complete failure. For the Egyptians it would be catastrophic, but for His People, it would guarantee them many good years to come. We are all acquainted with Joseph gathering all the grain that he could, and how he was used by God to keep both Egypt and his family alive; but we rarely take notice of how he did it! He had a strategy to make failure for one a success for the other.

Genesis 41: 56-57

'The famine was over all the face of the earth, and Joseph opened all the storehouses and sold to the Egyptians. And the famine became severe in the land of Egypt. So all countries came to Joseph in Egypt to buy grain, because the famine was severe in all lands.'

To secure the future of his family, Joseph had to tear the very fabric of Egyptian life. For his people to live in that land for a long time, the people of Egypt had to become poor, and they had to be uprooted from "life" as they knew it. With the help of the famine, Joseph adopted a policy of "Egyptian life failure" to accomplish that objective! For the people of God to live comfortably in Egypt for generations, all political power must be put into the hands of one man - Pharaoh. As long as he and succeeding Pharaoh's remembered Joseph and what he had done for the nation, they would live there securely. This policy by Joseph was put into action when the Egyptians started crying out to Pharaoh for bread. Joseph then began to sell the bread to them.

Genesis 47: 13-14

'Now there was no bread in all the land; for the famine was very severe, so that the land of Egypt and the land of Canaan languished because of the famine.
And Joseph gathered up all the money that was found in the land of Egypt and in the land of Canaan, for the grain which they bought; and Joseph brought the money into Pharaoh's house.'

The first phase of the purposeful downward spiral had now been completed. Pharaoh, under Joseph's hand, now had all the money. The second phase was now ready to implement.

Genesis 47: 15-17

'So when the money failed in the land of Egypt and in the land of Canaan, all the Egyptians came to Joseph and said, "Give us bread, for why should we die in your presence? For the money has failed."'
Then Joseph said, "Give your livestock, and I will give you bread for your livestock, if the money has gone." So they brought their livestock to Joseph, and Joseph gave them bread in exchange for the horses, the flocks, the cattle of the herds, and for the donkeys. Thus he fed them with the bread in exchange for all their livestock that year.

Joseph's policy of transferring the wealth of the Egyptians to Pharaoh had now completed its second phase. It took a year to fulfill the second phase but by the end of that year, the Egyptians had no money and no livestock. Pharaoh had it all.

Genesis 47: 18-20

'When that year had ended, they came to him the next year and said to him, "We will not hide from my lord that our money is gone; my lord also has our herds of livestock. There is nothing left in the sight of my lord but our bodies and our lands.

Why should we die before your eyes, both we and our land? Buy us and our land for bread, and we may live and not die, that the land may not be desolate."

Then Joseph bought all the land of Egypt for Pharaoh; for every man of the Egyptians sold his field, because the famine was severe upon them. So the land became Pharaoh's.'

Phase three of the Egyptian "road to failure" was now complete. Pharaoh was now in possession of all the money, all the livestock and all the land. On top of all that, apart from the priests of the land who were already under his control, every Egyptian was now under a kind of early feudal system where they tilled the land for their lord. To secure his family's future for the long-term, Joseph had only one thing more to do and that would finish the job. The final phase would now prove quite easy to accomplish because the once-vaunted people of Egypt who would previously look down their noses at shepherds, were now a spent force.

Genesis 47: 21

'And as for the people, he moved them into the cities from one end of the borders of Egypt to the other end.

Joseph broke the social and therefore the political power of Egyptian society. Not only were they all "flat broke" and owned nothing, they were forced to uproot from their homes and live in cities. By taking their money, their livestock and their land base, he secured the power of Pharaoh over the country and by so doing, secured the future for his people. (It's interesting to note that the Bible tells us that the Children of Israel's troubles began in Egypt when there arose a king who knew not Joseph.)

As far as Joseph was concerned the job was done, but just to be sure he added one more item to his list. He brought in a whole system of personal income tax for the Egyptians and the ratio that he used to calculate the tax is roughly what it is in most nations even today!

Genesis 47: 23-27

'Then Joseph said to the people, "Indeed I have bought you and your land this day for Pharaoh. Look, here is seed for you, and you shall sow the land. And it shall come to pass in the harvest that you shall give one-fifth to Pharaoh. Four-fifths shall be your own, as seed for the field and for your food, for those of your households and as food for your little ones."

So they said, "You have saved our lives; let us find favor in the sight of my lord, and we will be Pharaoh's servants."

And Joseph made it a law over the land of Egypt to this day, that Pharaoh should have one-fifth, except for the land of the priests only, which did not become Pharaoh's.

So Israel dwelt in the land of Egypt, in the country of Goshen: and they had possessions there and grew and multiplied exceedingly.'

In the previous example, we saw how the failure of Hagar's

water-bottle brought her into a new revelation of God's power and provision. God needed that water to be all used up before He could "open her eyes" to His supply.

In this example, the deliberate policy of Joseph to bring the Egyptians to total failure was God's way of securing His people's future under the hand of Pharaoh and his dynasty.

In a recent survey, it was found that for men in America; out of the ten things that they fear the most, the main one was failure. The thought of failure torments them more than anything else: more than going to the doctors; more than being wrong; even more than commitment. Failure - what a "giant" it has become in people's lives.

Nobody wants to fail - everybody wants to be successful! It's important to us to be seen as successful in life. We're constantly being told, "Don't be a loser! Don't even hang around with them! You never know what might rub off onto *you*!"

This wisdom of "When failure is success" is one of the most difficult principles to embrace and to even understand. Our Western minds have taught us that failure is final and in a sense it's like what Nathaniel said about Nazareth in that nothing good could come out of it! But God thinks differently about failure and He's not alone. Engineers have used the principle of "predictable failure" for years because they have discovered that when one system fails another one takes over. For example, the water sprinklers above our heads that extinguish office fires are designed on the principle of "predictable failure." Water sprinklers are not activated by smoke - they are activated by heat. Inside the sprinkler unit there is a small glass with glycerin inside and it has been designed to predictably fail when heated up. The glass is of such a gauge that when the glycerin reaches a certain temperature; the glass breaks, the water comes out, and the building is saved. Another example of "predictable failure" can be seen on our soda cans. When they first thought of putting soda into aluminum cans, the question was: "How does one open the can?" The engineers designed a weak spot in the top of the can so that when the tag was pulled, it would predictably fail and allow the consumer access to the soda. The design was further improved when they invented the "stay-tabs" that we're now familiar with because the old "throw-away tabs" would be found in clusters outside corner-shops and on beaches where they had become a real hazard.

In all of these things, failure has been the key to their success -predictable failure that is! So, here's an oxymoron for you to consider: "Failure works!" Failure works if you understand it.

The reason it doesn't work for most people is because the word "failure" conjures up so much anxiety that they can't think about it any other way outside of personal humiliation. They can't even look at it, never mind calculate with it! Predictable failure, if understood can be used for great service. It's one of God's unusual "doors" that allow Him to bring you into a world of difference!

This is the way that God brought into the world a brand-new creation. He arranged an "hour" of suffering for His Son to endure that would bear all the hallmarks of defeat. The Cross of Calvary was designed to bring Jesus to the point of "predictable failure" where even His followers would have all their hopes dashed. *We were hoping that it was He who was going to redeem Israel*" said one of them after He had been crucified.

And so it is for Christian men and women everywhere; they too must carry *their* Cross and endure its predictable failure. The Cross is not designed to lift us up. Resurrection is designed to lift us up! Jesus knew this and that's why He endured the Cross with all its apparent failure because great joy was waiting for Him after it. He knew that the "glass" of His life would break on it; but with the breaking of it, He was able to "sprinkle" many nations.

Without any fear of contradiction, we can all acknowledge that Christ in His death and subsequent resurrection is the greatest example we will ever have of "When failure is success."

Folks might say that failure of a predictable nature is one thing but failure that can be traced to personal culpability is quite another. This of course is very true, but even that kind of failure doesn't have to be the last word on a person's life or ministry.

One of the worst cases of failure is vividly portrayed for us in the life of Peter when he publicly denied knowing Jesus three times.

After having failed to identify himself with his Lord and Master he quickly left the scene and when he was alone he wept bitterly.

As he cried in the dark, the "giant" called "Personal Failure" came with his "club" and in all probability gave him a "rebuking session" that went something like this: "You idiot! You are history! What kind of future do you have now? Don't you get it? It's all over for you now. All that talk of you and the keys of the kingdom - forget about it! It's never going to happen. Let me repeat... You are done!"

However, failure was not the end because the Lord had a way for Peter to ascend out of his personal hell. One of the angels who appeared to the women on the resurrection morning gave them a message from the Lord that they were to tell His disciples *and* Peter, that they would *all* see Him in Galilee. Peter recovered from his failure because the Lord had forgiven him and put him on a path of restoration. After breakfast one morning, the Lord asked Peter three times about his love for Him and three times, Peter avowed his love. Jesus recommissioned him that day and his life and ministry were totally restored. Nothing had been lost and Peter was even better prepared for the work that he was called to.

I think it's safe to say that the whole experience laid a new foundation in him - a foundation that would last him for the rest of his life.

This example of the apostle Peter is not an isolated case. Did you ever read about the prophet Jonah who ran away from God and failed in his mission - how that the "word of the Lord" came to him a second time? I think that it's safe to say that his three days and three nights in the stomach of a whale laid a new foundation for the rest of his life too!

What makes us as Christians think twice about this subject is that the Bible is full of people who, even under the hand of God, have tasted of both success *and* failure! As we observe the dealings of God in their lives, we soon realize that success has not always been easily theirs. Life - even spiritual life, can be complicated. Having said that, we cannot allow the fear of failure to stop all our endeavors for God and we cannot afford for it to rob us from a healthy, questing spirit.

We know from the Scriptures that God is not impressed when His people stay behind the barriers of "safe success" and refuse to venture into "faith territory" with Him. "Safe success" is when we copy someone else's success and we pioneer no path of our own.

"Risk management" has its place within the fiduciary duties of "due diligence" but if we want to truly be successful in God we may have to leave the safety of the "river bank" and just follow Him into the river itself!

"What if I make a mistake and what if my efforts result in failure?" you may say. Those are relevant questions to ask but for the Christian the questions are more like: "What if I don't attempt anything for God? What will He say to me if at the end of my life, I have been like the one in the Bible, who buried his treasure in the ground?"

The Lord is not asking us to gamble with our lives, but He is expecting that from time to time we "step out in faith" and dare to do great things even when there is risk involved. Paul and Barnabas were men of great stature in the kingdom of God and the Bible says that they hazarded their lives for the Gospel!

Yes, they had set-backs but out of those failures came further successes. God enabled them to learn from them and turn their lessons into even more fruitful service.

During the First World War, it was well-documented that surgical knowledge had increased exponentially. Major advances in the area of wound treatments were recorded. This was because of the number of soldiers who were being brought into the field hospitals bearing wounds that the medical text-books had no reference for. Consequently, to save lives, the surgeons had to be very brave both to invent and perform new surgical techniques. Those new techniques were unproven and they presented great risk to the patients. The temptation for the doctors was to "play it safe" and not put the surgical staff at risk, but men were dying left and right, and so they did whatever they could to save them. They weren't always successful, but many procedures were, and they saved many lives because they had the "courage to fail."

We too must have the same mind because there is a Great War going on out there and people are dying in great numbers. Is it a time for us to "play it safe" and not put our lives at risk for those who are perishing? We must venture out and have the courage to even fail but if we do it in the right spirit we can fail successfully.

Our experience will be richer; our knowledge will be wider and our understanding of God will be deeper. If we dare to venture out with God, any mistakes that we do make; He is able to correct and any failures we encounter, He can draw success out of them. And even if He doesn't do any of those things, we will have been "the man in the arena" and when the books are opened in Heaven, the records will show that we pleased Him who called us.

Finally, there is one more aspect to this paradoxical truth of when "failure is success." As I mentioned before, failure always feels final, but sometimes, failure can be a *guarantee* of future success! There is a very famous city in America called Charleston. It was originally a bustling, wealthy city in what they call the 'The South.' By any stretch of the imagination, Charleston should now be counted among the country's greatest cities with a sprawling metropolis, but the American civil war changed its course when 'The South' was defeated. Charleston was "left to die" and places like Atlanta received the investments.

The high-rise apartments, the sky-scraper business blocks and the tall hotels were all built elsewhere, leaving Charleston locked in its past. Failure had come to the city. But as time went on, Charleston became an attraction *because* of its past failure, and people began to visit the city and enjoy its quaint surroundings.

It was so old-fashioned that it became a place for vacations, weddings and history buffs. There wasn't a high-rise building in sight and along with ancient houses and cobbled streets, Charleston became *the* place to visit! It wasn't long before the money returned and the real estate prices began to reflect the city's new-found success. Failure had put Charleston on lock-down for decades, but that failure kept the city in an antiquated condition, making it the very reason for its future success! Without that failure, Charleston would not be the success story that it is today!

So it is with God sometimes. He allows failure to visit, because He wants to preserve what's there for a new day in the future.

That's when Failure is Success!

WHEN LAST IS FIRST

Even a cursory look through the Gospels will bring the reader into some degree of familiarity with the paradoxical principle of "When last is first." Jesus used that phrase nearly ten times to annunciate this most important of truths concerning the Kingdom of God.

In this life, there are people who through their wealth and their social standing are considered to be the "first." Those who can afford "first-class" travel are the first to be seated, the first to be served and the first to leave. All over the world, the rich and the famous receive preferential treatment simply because they *are* rich and they *are* famous.

One day, as Jesus was teaching, a wealthy young man came running up to Him and knelt before Him. The young man was an expert in the law and he had lived according to its commands yet remained unsure as to his eternal destiny. "Good Teacher" he said. "What good thing shall I do that I may have eternal life?" Jesus reiterated the precepts of the law to him to which he affirmed his personal keeping of them. "What do I still lack" he said. Jesus said to him, "If you want to be perfect; go, sell what you have and give to the poor, and you will have treasure in heaven; and come, follow Me."

When the young man heard those words, he got up and left with a sad heart because he had great possessions. "How hard it is for a rich man to enter the kingdom of heaven!" Jesus told the crowd.

This whole conversation provoked a response in Peter who said to the Lord: "Look, we have left everything and followed You. Therefore, what shall we have?" The Lord began to assure Peter that he and anyone like him who would leave everything to follow Him, would receive huge blessings in this life *and* in the life to come. But then the Lord added this thought to the words that He had just said: "But many who are first will be last, and the last first." He then began to speak a parable about the Kingdom of God and in order to give it some context, He used the principle of "When last is first" as its two "book-ends."

Matthew 20: 1 – 16

"For the kingdom of heaven is like a land-owner who went out early in the morning to hire laborers for his vineyard. Now when he had agreed with the laborers for a denarius a day, he sent them into his vineyard.

And he went out about the third hour and saw others standing idle in the marketplace and said to them 'You also go into the vineyard, and whatever is right I will give you.' So they went.

Again he went out about the sixth hour and the ninth hour, and did likewise.

And about the eleventh hour he went out and found others standing idle, and said to them, 'Why have you been standing here idle all day?' They said to him, 'Because no one hired us.' He said to them, 'You also go into the vineyard, and whatever is right you will receive.'

So when the evening had come, the owner of the vineyard said to his steward, 'Call the laborers and give them their wages, beginning with the last to the first.' And when those came who were hired about the eleventh hour, they received a denarius.

But when the first came, they supposed that they would receive more; and they likewise received a denarius. And when they had received it, they complained against the landowner, saying, 'These last men have worked only one hour and you have made them equal to us who have borne the burden and the heat of the day.'

But he answered one of them and said, 'Friend, I am doing you no wrong. Did you not agree with me for a denarius? Take what is yours and go your way. I wish to give to this last man the same as you. Is it not lawful for me to do what I wish with my own things? Or is your eye evil because I am good?

"So the last will be first, and the first last. For many are called, but few are chosen."

Jesus spoke this parable in light of Peter's comments for I think that the Lord had detected a wrong spirit in what he'd said.

The initial application of this parable has Almighty God as the "landowner" who has from eternity called both Jews and Gentiles into His "vineyard" but His calling has come at different times. If this parable has a hidden *historical* narrative, it shows that the Jews were the first to be called into the vineyard. They answered that call and served the Lord in His vineyard over many years. But then, towards the end of God's dispensations, the Gospel of His grace was presented to the Gentiles so that they too could be called to work in the vineyard. Not only should they be admitted; they should enjoy equal privileges with the Jews and become fellow-citizens of the Kingdom of Heaven. Jesus told His own people that *"many will come from the east and west and sit down with Abraham, Isaac and Jacob in the Kingdom of Heaven."* That is one application of this parable in which we can understand redemptive history.

But this parable of Jesus brings a more *personal* application to us in that we can *all* fit into this story in one way or another.

This parable highlights a particular temptation that comes to those who have been Christians for a long time - even from a child.

There's no part of the Christian life without its dangers.

Temptations to go back into the world come to the newly-saved, but for the mature in Christ, the temptations have to be much more subtle than that. And indeed they are.

Firstly, let me say that it's very important to have a good start in your Christian life. There's no substitute for a complete "turn-around" kind of conversion, but we must have the heart to go on and this parable comes as a reminder to the old saints; that they must continue on in the right attitude or if they're not careful, the very grace that blessed their lives so many years ago can become an irritant towards those who've only been saved "five minutes." The temptation to envy others is a very powerful one and the "root of jealousy" is deeper in us than what we may think!

This parable tells us of people coming into the vineyard at different times of a twelve hour day. Applying it to believers, it first speaks of those who were called when they were young. As children or youth, they were called to the vineyard of the Kingdom "early in the morning" of their lives.

Others were called by God in their middle age years and they came into the vineyard at the third, sixth and ninth hours. Then there are those who are hired at the "eleventh hour" of their lives and they were called to work in the vineyard in their old age; in their later years.

Did you notice that nobody is hired at the twelfth hour? At that time, life is over and when life is over, opportunity to work in the vineyard is not available; but "where there is *life*, there is hope." There is hope for old sinners - men and women whose hearts have been hardened over a life-time can *still* go into the vineyard! There's *still* time to serve and there's *still* space available! But there is a warning here to anyone who would seek to get themselves "right with God" only when they're old or dying. These last ones were sent into the vineyard because no man had hired them. In other words, it wasn't their fault. They *would* have been working had they been called earlier! So, here is a lesson to be learned: death-bed salvations may be the glory of God's mercy but they are the worst gamble in the world! Always remember this: two thieves were crucified with Jesus - one was saved so that all may have hope, but only one, that none may presume! Repentance is a gift from God and you just can't "turn it on" when you think you need it! We must never presume on the grace of God like that.

Let's go back to the parable.

Eventually, the working day came to an end and the laborers were then called to the steward to be paid. Interestingly, the steward was instructed to call the last ones first so that they would be paid first. The steward gave them their wages. They received every man, a denarius, which was a Roman coin equivalent to a fair day's pay.

One can only imagine what must have been going through the minds of those who had been working in the vineyard from six o'clock that morning when they saw those who had just arrived receiving a denarius - a full day's wage! *"Wow, if he's paid those men a full day's wage, what are we going to get?"* (Like Peter, who said to Jesus, "We've left everything to follow You; therefore, what shall we have?") Then the story became really interesting because *every* man received a full day's pay. They *all* got the *same* wages! The early workers were offended by this and they complained against the landowner because everything in them was crying out, "This is not fair."

When we encounter an unfair situation, it's human nature to want to blame somebody for that, and it's never too long before the sentence changes from *"This* is not fair" to *"You* are not fair!" They complained against *him* - the landowner; the good man of the house - and he responded.

"Friend, I am doing you no wrong. Did you not agree with me for a denarius? Take what is yours and go your way. I wish to give to this last man the same as you."

When these men were hired early in the morning, they were glad to have the work and they were content with the pay scale offered to them. All that evaporated when they saw those whom they thought were unworthy, receive unmerited favor from the landowner. (They became like the elder brother in the 'Prodigal Son' story who complained to his father concerning his generosity towards his unworthy younger brother!) As for these first workers, they weren't complaining about their wages, for they had an agreement. They quarreled with the landowner because he had made the last ones *equal* to them! This to them was unfair!

"We have born the burden and the heat of the day and these men just came in the last hour and you have made them the same as us!"

(Have you noticed something about ourselves as humans; that we can easily undervalue what *others* have done and yet overvalue what *we* have done, and feel deserving of even more?)

The master of the house disagreed with those first workers, saying, *"Friend, I have done you no wrong. Am I not honoring our agreement? Did you not agree with me for a denarius?"*

Those men only went to work *after* an agreement but the others *all* went to work when the landowner said to them: *"Go into the vineyard and I will give you whatever is right."* The first ones it would seem had a tendency to strike a bargain; to make certain demands and conditions. If I am wrong in this deduction, it's certain that they were *very* conscious of what they had done and how long they had done it for! What a terrible thing "self" is sometimes! But are we not all guilty of it in some way; watching ourselves; keeping mental records of everything we've done; how long we've prayed; how much we've given, etc.?

These early workers knew it all – the *many* hours that they had done and the *few* hours that the others had done. They felt that they were entitled to more because they had done more - a logical conclusion for the natural man - but not with the Lord. This is a parable showing us a facet of the Kingdom of Heaven and that facet is this, if you haven't already worked it out: that the Kingdom of God is not earned - it's given! *"It is the Father's good pleasure to give you the Kingdom."*

What happened to these *last* workers was this: grace came into their lives. They did not deserve a full day's pay but because the landowner was good, they received the benefits of his grace.

What a joy it must have been for them in that moment. All of them would have returned home to their wives saying: "Honey, you would *not* believe what happened this evening!"

The problem with the first workers is that they didn't understand the grace of the landowner. They understood "works" but they did not understand "grace." As a result, the joy of receiving wages went out of them and misery took over. They became jealous of those who had been blessed and they became very upset with the one who had blessed them!

As was mentioned earlier, this shows a particular kind of temptation that comes to the old saint; to the mature believer; to the one who has been working in the vineyard for many years; perhaps all their lives. It's the impulse of jealousy that comes against those who've been recently saved and have only been in the church the proverbial "five minutes" whom the Lord has chosen to bless greatly. This temptation comes to the mature in subtle ways and it makes them feel quite miserable because they feel that others have been rewarded for just for showing up! A strong, negative feeling arises in their hearts that says: "The landowner is unjust." Having served God for many years there comes a sense of entitlement that echoes the sentiments of those first workers who *supposed that they should have more.*

In the parable of the 'Prodigal Son' there came a similar moment when the elder brother complained to his father about the whole "fatted calf" and "party" thing. But do you remember what the father said to his eldest son? He said some very precious words to him.

"Son, you are always with me and everything I have is yours."

Allow me to remind you, that the Father whom you worship, is so generous; that you can go into His vineyard and work for Him and be blessed more than you will *ever* deserve! You do not have to strike a bargain with Him. If you strike a bargain with God, that's exactly what you will receive - a bargain, but no more! It'll work out so much better for you if you will gladly go into the vineyard and believe that He will give to you whatever is right in His eyes!

The Kingdom of Heaven is a world where grace is the only currency; the only legal tender; and grace blows all earthly principles away, and turns the world upside down - or should I say, turns the world the right way up?

In this world of works and effort, it doesn't make any sense to have the last come first, but in the Kingdom of God, it makes perfect sense because whatever "hour" of your life in which you were called into the vineyard, it is *all* of God's grace! If you got saved when you were young - that was God's grace. If you got saved in your mid-life - that was God's grace. And if you came to know the Lord at the twilight of your life - that was God's grace too!

This parable shows us that God gives His rewards through sovereign grace and not of debt. God is indebted to no man. We are indebted to *Him*, for "all have sinned and come short of the glory of God. There is no one righteous; no not even one!"

Our salvation and our rewards are based upon Him who calls us to Himself and bids us to go work in His vineyard. The truth is that none of us deserve wages for even when we *do* work for Him, it's like the apostle Paul said: *"I labored, yet not I, but the grace of God that was with me."*

Having told them this parable, He concluded with the thoughts with which He had begun: *"So the last shall be first, and the first last. For many are called, but few chosen."*

There is a *common call* to everyone who hears the Gospel and those who *do* respond; those who go into the vineyard of God; soon discover that the general call that they heard was actually an *effectual call* in their personal lives. Many people have heard the Gospel of God, which is the message that can save them; but for whatever reason, they have chosen *not* to respond and go into the vineyard. At the end of their lives they will realize that they were called with a "common call" but they had not been chosen with God's saving choice! There are many people in the world that call themselves Christians but there are fewer chosen Christians, whom the Bible describes as having been born again. These are those who have been baptized into Christ through repentance of sins and confession of faith and are the happy recipients of the Holy Spirit.

In light of this parable of God's grace, what will prove to be the most important thing on Judgement Day is that *whatever* age you were called, you *did* respond to God and you *did* go and work in His vineyard. If you came in young, praise the Lord. If you came in later, praise the Lord; and if you came in at the "eleventh hour" - praise the Lord! It's His *grace* upon your life that counts. As for your eternal rewards, the Lord will give you whatever is right.

You won't be disappointed!

As Abraham said to the Lord one time, *"Shall not the Judge of all the earth do right?"* God will always do the right thing by you and His grace towards *you* ... is amazing!

DECLARATIONS BEFORE THE FACT

One of the mysteries of God lies in the fact that He is outside the scope of our time. The Scriptures tell us that He is the God Who was, Who is and Who is to come! The Lord Jesus Christ told the apostle John in the Book of Revelation that He was the Alpha and the Omega, the First and the Last. Even when Jesus was among us, He said: "Before Abraham was - I Am."

What these truths mean to us in a *practical* way is that before we reach our destination, God is already there! He is with us *before* we "run" - He is with us *when* "run" and He is at the finishing line when we *finish* the "run."

What these truths mean for us in a *spiritual* way is that because God knows the end from the beginning, He can speak predictively into our lives about things that will happen in the future. Indeed, one of the things that the Holy Spirit has been commissioned to do is to "show us things to come." It is therefore in the nature of God to speak prophetically and declare things before they become facts. He rules all things through fiat and that through His decrees, He fulfills His desires.

The whole creation was brought to birth in this manner when God said, "Let there be light" and there was light. He spoke - and it was! He brought all things into being and then He called them what He desired. The only exception to this was the first man. Adam was given the prerogative of naming the woman that God gave to him, and all the animal kingdom, including the birds of the air.

Let's take a look at our first example of God decreeing things over people's lives even before they "ran" their race.

Genesis 25: 21- 24

'Now Isaac pleaded with the Lord for his wife, because she was barren; and the Lord granted his plea, and Rebekah his wife conceived. But the children struggled together within her; and she said "If all is well, why am I like this?" So she went to inquire of the Lord.

And the Lord said to her: "Two nations are in your womb; Two peoples shall be separated from your body; One people shall be stronger than the other and the older shall serve the younger."

So when her days were fulfilled for her to give birth, indeed there were twins in her womb.'

The New Testament goes on to give a further account of this moment when it tells us of the elective purposes of God - purposes that are able to prevail over human life and will.

Romans 9: 10-12

'But when Rebekah had conceived by one man, even our father Isaac (for the children not yet being born, nor having done any good or evil, that the purpose of God according to election might stand, not of works but of Him who calls), it was said to her, "The older shall serve the younger."

Before Jacob and Esau were born, God declared their futures. From a human point of view this seems very unfair but God is past, present and future and therefore He knows what will take place and moreover He has planned what will take place. In fact, the Bible tells us that God has finished all His works way back in the eternal past! That means He can "declare things before they happen" and it also means that He's never taken by surprise!

What is prophetic to us is establishment to Him. The fiat word of God is known as "the word of promise" and He is faithful to fulfill His promises. When Abraham and his wife Sarah were too old to conceive, the Lord said to Abraham: *"I have made you a father of many nations."* It looked impossible for that to take place at that time of their lives, but God can call into existence things that are presently not there and act as if they were! In simple terms it means that if God has said it, it will happen. He can declare things *before* they become facts! This is how He operates in people's lives and in their work in the Kingdom. Those who are called to be prophets understand this principle more than most because they are used by God to speak out His decrees. Let's observe this dynamic in the ministry of God's word in the prophet Ezekiel.

Ezekiel 2: 7-10 & Ezekiel 3: 1- 4

'"You shall speak My words to them, whether they hear or whether they refuse, for they are rebellious. But you, son of man, hear what I say to you, Do not be rebellious like that rebellious house; open your mouth and eat what I give you."

Now when I looked, there was a hand stretched out to me; and behold, a scroll of a book was in it. Then He spread it before me; and there was writing on the inside and on the outside, and written on it were lamentations and mourning and woe.

Moreover He said to me, "Son of man, eat what you find; eat this scroll, and go, speak to the house of Israel."

So I opened my mouth, and He caused me to eat that scroll. And He said to me, "Son of man, feed your belly, and fill your stomach with this scroll that I give you." So I ate, and it was in my mouth like honey in sweetness.

Then He said to me: Son of man, go to the house of Israel and speak with My words to them."'

Here is a wonderful example of how God brings His will into the world through the revelation of His fiat word. He commits His intentions to His ministers who are then commanded to speak them out. Until the prophet speaks them out the words will remain as an "intention of God" but once they are delivered through the mouth of the Minister they become alive and effective. The words "jump off the paper" so to speak and they become active in the arena to which they were sent. At that point, the message is delivered and the "papers" are served. The words that had once been declared as the "divine intention" are now "at the door" and no man can shut it! The words then become reality and the will of God is done.

The statement "before the fact" is a legal phrase which speaks of the actual event. And what we're talking about here are the decisions and the declarations of God *before* the event happens. When you've been a Christian for some time, you soon begin to understand that before anything happens in *this* world, it has already been decided in the *other* world; the invisible, spiritual world, where God's Throne is. This understanding doesn't come easily or quickly to us, but as life goes on, we become increasingly aware that God and His Providence are ruling not only over *our* lives, but also the affairs of men and nations. We eventually come to realize that it is *His* decisions and *His* declarations that determine outcomes. Let us put it this way: *"God declares, then we tell it, then it's done!* He is a God who declares things before the fact; before the event; and then makes sure it's accomplished.

1 Kings 17: 8-9

'Then the word of the Lord came to him (Elijah), saying, "Arise, go to Zarephath, which belongs to Sidon, and dwell there. See, I have commanded a widow there to provide for you."

In the normal context of human understanding, we would think that this statement is in the past tense and that it is now a declaration of present fact. It reads as though God had already spoken to this particular widow to sustain Elijah, and that she knew all about it and would have everything ready for his arrival. But that was not the case. When God was speaking these words to Elijah, the widow had no idea what God had decided to do. This was one of God's prophetic statements; one of His declarations before the fact. There's a lot we can say about this event, but what is important for us to understand is that the decision by God to use this woman to sustain Elijah had taken place *before* the woman knew or even perceived of it. The decision was made in Heaven; declared to the prophet on earth and then accomplished in the world. The widow complied.

Let me give you one more example of this principle of God's sovereignty at work. Let's read about king Cyrus, the pagan king of Persia; whom God raised up to fulfill His will; to rebuild Jerusalem and its Temple.

Isaiah 44: 28 & Isaiah 45: 1-6

'Who says of Cyrus, 'He is My shepherd, and he shall perform all My pleasure, saying to Jerusalem, "You shall be built," and to the temple, "Your foundation shall be laid."'

"Thus says the Lord to His anointed, to Cyrus, whose right hand I have held - to subdue nations before him and loose the armor of kings, to open before him the double doors, so that the gates will not be shut: 'I will go before you and make the crooked places straight; I will break in pieces the gates of bronze and cut the bars of iron. I will give you the treasures of darkness and hidden riches of secret places, that you may know that I, the Lord, Who call you by your name, am the God of Israel.

For Jacob My servant's sake, and Israel My elect, I have called you by your name; I have named you, though you have not known Me. I am the Lord, and there is no other; There is no God besides Me. I will gird you, though you have not known Me."'

These words spoken by the prophet Isaiah were spoken two hundred years before king Cyrus was around to be shown them! At the time these words were declared, Jerusalem was functioning as the capital city and the Temple priests were fulfilling their sacerdotal ceremonies. However, God was annunciating that day through Isaiah some "declarations before the events" and speaking prophetically, He gave the man who was to come, the name Cyrus, and predetermined what He would do! Before Cyrus was born, God had already decided his destiny. Truly we can say: *"God decides, God declares, God does!"*

God brought Cyrus into world history to do His will and fulfill what the Scriptures had declared about him. By reading this prophecy of Isaiah, king Cyrus would understand why he had been made the most powerful man on earth at that time. Those words that were spoken about him so long ago would have given him a great awareness that Heaven's decrees are much higher than his! He would understand that the Great God, is the God of Israel and that he was put in his position to "open the door" for God's people to return back to Jerusalem and build the Temple.

Let me put it plainly - God is always a step ahead!

Let us now apply this principle of God to us, for although these things may seem strange and unusual, declaring things before they take place is common sense to the God who is Alpha and Omega in our lives.

Isaiah 42: 5-9

"Behold, the former things have come to pass, and new things I declare; Before they spring forth I tell you of them."

'Sing to the Lord a new song, and His praise from the ends of the earth; You who go down to the sea, and all that is in it; You coastlands and you inhabitants of them!

Let the wilderness and its cities lift up their voice; The villages that Kedar inhabits. Let the inhabitants of Sela sing, let them shout from the top of the mountains. Let them give glory to the Lord and declare His praise in the coastlands.

The Lord shall go forth like a mighty man; He shall stir up His zeal like a man of war. He shall cry out, yes, shout aloud; He shall prevail against His enemies.'

Here is one of God's declarations before the fact. Verse nine says: "New things I declare; *before* they spring forth, I tell you of them." Before things happen; before events take place, God declares them and tells us about them! God declares today, what He's already decided to do in the past, about what He's going to do in the future! To put this another way; God is saying, "I am going to tell you *today* what I decided *yesterday* to do *tomorrow*! It's going to spring forth soon, but it's already been in existence in My mind, and I want to tell you about it now!"

The interpretation of these verses is to be seen in the context of what God was saying to His people Israel at that time; but I am persuaded that these words have a prophetic application to us, here and now. These Scriptures speak of the whole world being touched with the salvation of God, where people of every clime and culture will sing out a new song to the Lord. It is the song of the redeemed of the Lord - those who have been saved through the Gospel His grace. We are now in the time when His praise can be sung from one end of the earth to the other. Please notice that it's not *our* praise that is sent forth - it's *His* praise that is sung around the world. The song of God's salvation is to "belt the globe" for God declared to His Son centuries ago that the nations would be His inheritance and that the ends of the earth would be His possession. This "word of promise" was given to Jesus, long before Calvary's Cross and subsequent resurrection. These promises were given to Jesus by God, and they were written in the Scriptures - and the Scriptures cannot fail! Christ will see the "travail" of His soul and be satisfied, because they will come to Him out of every tribe, tongue and nation and He will rule them.

The peoples of the far-east; China, Japan and the Korea's will be included with the western nations of the United States and Canada. The "song of salvation" will touch all those countries on the skirts of the Arctic Circle like Russia, Finland and Scandinavia and it will be heard in the south in places like Chile, Argentina, Australia and South Africa. These Scriptures talk about those whose livelihoods are found in the fishing fields of the seas; of those living by coastlands and in island communities. Even those who live in the remote cities of the desert, the inhabitants of the wilderness; even they will sing a new song and lift up their voice to the Lord! It mentions the tent villages of Kedar who are represented by those nomadic tribes who are always on the move - they too will sing a new song as they travel from place to place. This song of the Lord's salvation will reach the mountain peoples of Sela who are represented by those who live in cities of high elevation. They also will shout the salvation of God from the top of their mountains. *Everyone* will give glory to the Lord and declare His praise! All of these things will happen because the Lord declared that He was going to stir Himself up and go forth like a mighty man of war.

He promised to cry out aloud and prevail against His enemies and that is exactly what He did when Jesus in the last moment of His life, cried aloud those magnificent words: "It is finished!"

Yes, the Lord is a 'Man of War' and He defeated all His enemies at the Cross. It was then when God's "declaration before the fact" spoken to Eve in the Garden, was fulfilled as Jesus "bruised the serpent's head" in the darkness of that hour.

What has God declared over your life? What promises do you believe He has spoken to you? Everyone's life is unique and therefore the "blue-print" for every child of God is different but whatever our personal call entails, we must remember that we are all in the "harvest" together. That means we must all be found in the "field" of the world; bringing the saving message of the Gospel of Christ to the islands, to the coastlands, to the deserts, to the mountains. Wherever the children of men are - there we must be willing to go.

Success is not fulfilling *our* vision for our lives. Success is fulfilling *God's* vision for our lives! Success is discovering and obediently living out *His* declarations over our lives. It's an exciting life!

STRANGE THINGS

We don't have to travel down the road of life too far before we begin to encounter unusual and strange things. For children and youth who have known their parent's love and security, life in the main, is sweetly predictable. As we grow older however, things that are foreign and unfamiliar break into our lives - sometimes from unusual quarters. We are then, as they say, "side-swiped" because that which has not been previously known or expected is now apparent. We all like new things and new experiences but we can all become a little nervous when those events are odd, quirky or highly unusual. Life as we know it holds "surprise packages" of all different kinds and some of them can only be described as "very strange indeed." This chapter looks at some of the strange things that God has done. They were strange to men but not to Him!

Luke 5: 17- 26

'Now it happened on a certain day, as He was teaching, that there were Pharisees and teachers of the law sitting by, who had come out of every town of Galilee, Judea, and Jerusalem. And the power of the Lord was present to heal them.

Then behold, men brought on a bed a man who was paralyzed, whom they sought to bring in and lay before Him. And when they could not find how they might bring him in, because of the crowd, they went up on the housetop and let him down with his bed through the tiling into the midst before Jesus.

When He saw their faith, He said to him, "Man, your sins are forgiven you." And the scribes and the Pharisees began to reason, saying, "Who is this who speaks blasphemies? Who can forgive sins but God alone?"

But when Jesus perceived their thoughts, He answered and said to them, "Which is easier to say, 'Your sins are forgiven you,' or to say 'Rise up and walk'? But that you may know that the Son of Man has power on earth to forgive sins" - He said to the man who was paralyzed, "I say to you, arise, take up your bed, and go to your house."

Immediately, he rose up before them, took up what he had been lying on, and departed to his own house, glorifying God. And they were all amazed, and they glorified God and were filled with fear, saying "We have seen strange things today!"

There are two aspects to this topic of "strange things" that need to be understood. First, there *are* some "strange things" that God has a problem with; and secondly, there *are* some "strange things" that have God's signature written all over them. We're not talking about "two sides of the one coin" - we are dealing with two different *sources* and therefore two different *worlds*. So, before we look at these two different worlds, let us first reflect on the immutability of God's unchanging character; Who from His throne, rules all things, strange or otherwise.

With respect to His character, God is the same; yesterday, today and forever! *"I am the Lord"* He says, *"I change not."*

What that means to us in a practical way is that while God *is* almighty, He still governs Himself through the holiness of His laws and by the principles of His light. He will never step outside the statutes of His laws and He has bound Himself to stand by everything He says. In fact, He's magnified His Word above His own Name, so that it will be more possible for heaven and earth to pass away than for His Word to fail! His heart is fixed in righteousness to the point where it is impossible for Him to lie.

He *won't* do it. He *can't* do it! All these things tell us that where God's character is involved, and where our fellowship with Him is experienced; we will always find God to be just as His Word declares. The truth found in the Scriptures mirrors the Truth that He is. Believing rightly what the Bible clearly says about Him is called Orthodox Christianity. "Orthodox" is a combination of two words: "ortho" meaning "correct" and "doxa" meaning "belief" or "thought."

If anyone says they truly know God, they will have a sound Biblical view of Him. They will have the right opinion about God because they will have the correct belief. Those who believe right will be orthodox in the essential things of God, Christ, and the way of salvation. So, Orthodox Christianity can be described as "conforming to the *approved form* of any Christian doctrine" concerning the nature of God and His redemptive work in Jesus Christ. "Orthodoxy" can also be described as a *customary* or *conventional means* to that which has been *established*. The opposite of this is called "heterodox" or "unorthodox" and for this study we will refer to those things as "strange."

There are things that God counts as strange, because they are foreign to His character and to His ways.

Genesis 35: 2 and Deuteronomy 32: 12 & 16 are all references to "strange gods" and how that they had no place in the lives of the People of God. In Exodus 30: 9 the Lord reminded the priests to do everything as He had commanded, in that they were not to offer "strange incense" from off the altar.

Leviticus 10: 1-3 and Numbers 3: 4 talks about the "strange fire" that two of the sons of Aaron had offered to God and had died before the Lord, presuming to do that which God had not commanded them. 1Kings 11: 1 talks about all the foreign (strange) wives that King Solomon took for himself, and there are many admonitions in the Proverbs for men to be aware of the "strange" woman.

Now it has to be said that the old covenant had a more prescribed way of doing things, because the People of God were then under Law and subject to ceremonial Law. The liberty of grace and truth came later with Jesus Christ and that's why new covenant believers can now enjoy the freedom that comes in Him. New covenant believers have been totally justified and they are now the Children of God! However, the New Testament still warns us about "strange" things. There is a warning in the Book of Jude for those who maintain unrighteous lives to remember the fate of the men of Sodom and Gomorrah, who gave themselves over to "strange flesh." However, the one we all have to be aware of the most - because it affects the most, is written for us in Hebrews 13: 9 when it says, *"Do not be carried about by various and strange doctrines."*

1 Timothy 4: 1-7

'Now the Spirit expressly says that in the latter times some will depart from the faith, giving heed to deceiving spirits and doctrines of demons, speaking lies in hypocrisy, having their own conscience seared with a hot iron, forbidding to marry, and commanding to abstain from foods which God created to be received with thanksgiving by those who believe and know the truth. For every creature of God is good, and nothing is to be refused if it is received with thanksgiving; for it is sanctified by the word of God and prayer.

If you instruct the brethren in these things, you will be a good minister of Jesus Christ, nourished in the words of faith and of good doctrine which you have carefully followed.

But reject profane and old wives' fables, and exercise yourself toward godliness.'

What Paul is revealing here is that the times that usher in the end of the age will be marked by a lot of deception and many will stop being Christians and leave the Faith. They will do this because they have been deceived by *unorthodox teachings* having to do with God, His ways and His Word. The apostle is saying that in the Last Days, many strange doctrines will be embraced. Some of them will be very wrong; others, simply unorthodox in that historically speaking, they were never viewed as part of normal Christian teaching or expression - whatever denomination people adhered to!

Let me share with you *some* things that are accepted now; that in nearly two thousand years of Church history, have never fallen into the generally approved form of Christian doctrine and life. Not *all* the things mentioned here are intrinsically evil - just strange - a bit "foreign" you might say.

1. There's a teaching making great strides in Christianity today which says that once you've repented for your salvation, you will never have to do it again. You'll never have to get down on your knees again and ask God to forgive you; to cleanse you; to restore you; because He did that for you at the Cross.

While there's an aspect of truth within that doctrine, it remains unsupported by the balance and weight of the New Testament Scriptures. It's strange because it's a foreign view to orthodox Christianity.

2. There's a teaching prevailing today that you can live an active homosexual lifestyle and be a Christian all at the same time!

The New Testament tells us not to be deceived even in matters like these, for the unrighteous will not inherit the Kingdom of God.

3. There's an old teaching that has gained a lot of traction in recent years. It's the one that says: *"You can be a Christian without going to Church."*

This teaching has promoted non-attendance at the House of God in all denominations. It has weakened the numerical strength of the local church and has syphoned off much of the financial flow that was destined for the "storehouses" of Christ.

This practice is unbiblical, unorthodox and sadly, not new.

4. Both Ministers and congregants today have taken a very casual approach to how they dress for Church.

In most denominations in the past; if the Ministers of Christ didn't wear robes or gowns, they would at least wear a suit.

Historically, in both Old and New testament settings, the main thought behind people's attendance at the temple or the church was for them to *"present themselves before God."* When I was young, I saw many people step inside the church and the first thing they did when they found their seat, was to bow their heads and pray. They would be horrified now to see how casual we've all become! A casual approach to church services isn't necessarily evil - just strange. For many older saints, it's "historically strange" for people not to bow before the Lord and pray when they come into His Presence.

5. For two thousand years of Church history and at least fifteen hundred years of Judaism; God and light went together. Whenever people worshiped God, they would do it in the light. Candle-light was always a feature of worship because God was in the Holy Place and God *is* light, and in Him there is no darkness at all. So why has much of this generation embraced the notion that worshiping God in the dark, is congruent for Divine service; especially when historically, it was the séances that were conducted in the dark?

As I said before, not necessarily evil - just strange.

6. There's a subtle teaching abroad today that says: "If you really want to be blessed by God, you must embrace the Jewishness of the Faith by accepting some of the forms and practices of the old covenantal system - a kind of "Messianic Judaism." In many churches today, it's not unusual to see a model of the ark of the covenant right in the middle of the platform along with congregants wearing prayer shawls and blowing shofars. Some churches now have their interior walls painted in the colors of the Old Testament Tabernacle.

All of those things are unorthodox concerning the New Covenant doctrines of Christ. All of them! They all belong to a covenant arrangement in which God found inherent weakness and so He took it away; making all those pre-requisites of Judaism obsolete. As I said, not necessarily evil - but definitely strange! "Messianic Judaism" is a contradiction in terms! Grace and Law are two different ways of living and they are two different positions before God. We must be very careful not to send "grace" out of the "back door" and welcome in the old relics through the front!

These then, are just some of the "strange things" that we who are living in these times must watch out for and be prepared to examine. "How" - you may ask?" We examine all things by the Word of God that never fails and by the Spirit of God Who never changes. All teachings and expressions of the Christian Faith must be congruent with the Holy Scriptures for the Holy Spirit will not contradict today what He inspired men to write yesterday!

Now, let's take a look at the *other* aspect of "strange things" which is the great and glorious part. In this aspect, God, in His marvelous workmanship, is not bound at all! In His ability to create, He is unlimited! The expanse of His power is beyond all human minds. As the Bible says: *"The Heaven of heavens cannot contain Him."*

The text that was at the head of this chapter was about the incident that Jesus had with the paralyzed man, when He forgave all his sins and raised him up to walk again. What a reaction Jesus received from the people who heard and saw what He did!

'And they were all amazed, and they glorified God and were filled with fear, saying, "We have seen strange things today!"

To put it in today's colloquial language - they'd never seen anything like it! Jesus was constantly saying and doing things that were incredible. Searching through the Gospel accounts of the Lord and His ministry, I found that the word "amaze" or "amazed" was there sixteen times. I found the word "wonder" or "wondered" fourteen times and I found the word "marvel" or "marveled" twenty times!

The Bible is full of the wonders of God. Incredible things

are written about Him and not only Him, but those who stepped out in faith and dared to believe in Him! When they "put their hand in God's hand" they walked through this life with the God in Whom *all* things are possible! One of the disciples even walked on water! Now, that's strange!

As was mentioned in the introduction to this book, there's a lot of talk these days about "thinking outside the box" or "doing things outside the box." From a creative point of view, it's a very healthy philosophy, as long as you don't end up despising the box! Consider this: you can only "think outside the box" if there *is* a box to think outside *of!* You *need* the box so you can think *outside* of it!

But what do people generally mean when they talk this way? What is the message that comes across? The message is that the "box" is for people who live in "Normalsville.' The "box" is for those who are conservative, conventional and perhaps a little dull. The world outside the "box" is for those with creative genius; for those with flair; for those who can bring something new to the table.

I believe that God is fine with life inside *or* outside the box because He lives according both! He's amazing inside *and* outside of it! To use another analogy, God has created a solid river-bed upon which flows the River of His Holy Spirit. That River will flow wherever God's pre-determined river-bed allows, and in seasons where it overflows its banks, its momentum and direction still remain in the current of the general direction.

The Scriptures are God's "river-bed" and the Holy Spirit is the "River." He can flood whole regions with signs and wonders; where people who come under His influence will say to each other: "We have never seen anything like it!" Many strange and wonderful things can take place but everything

He does will have its foundation in the "river-bed" of God's Word.

This is called "balance." God wants you to be able to stand in the *conventional doctrines* of the New Testament and yet be flexible enough to believe God for *unconventional miracles.* Let me put it another way. On *essential* Christian doctrine, you must be firmly in the orthodox "ball-park" and then, in matters of creativity, you can knock the ball anywhere you want! You can even knock it *out* of the park as long as your feet are on the "plate" of solid ground. When you believe correctly, anything you do that is creative *will* glorify God. When your Christian beliefs are faulty, your "out of the box" creativity runs the risk of becoming a little bizarre! We should always be willing to embrace the new and the different, but we must always watch out for the bizarre.

So, feel free to think "outside the box" as you understand it, but please remember that with God, even "inside the box" is - as John Denver used to say back in the Seventies – "Far out!"

God's box is *very* big! Here are some things that were done by Him and His people inside *His* box - inside the marvelous conventions of His Word: -

Miracles in the land of Egypt - snakes, frogs, lice, darkness, death! The parting of the Red Sea and the Jordan River. The walls of the city of Jericho falling down flat. The sun standing still for Joshua until he defeated his enemies. A donkey speaking to a disobedient prophet. The sending of ravens with food morning and evening to feed his servant Elijah. Miracles with flour and oil in Elisha's life. Samson's unbelievable strength as he pulls up the gates of a city and carries them away to the top of a hill. Miraculous escape from hungry lions. A disobedient prophet kept alive in the belly of a whale. Ax heads rising to the surface of water. Walking on water. Lepers being cleansed; healing the sick; raising people back to life! Need I go on?

All of these things happened within the scope of God's box! If He can do these things inside the "ball-park" of His Word; what can He creatively do outside the park?

The tracks of New Testament Christianity have been firmly laid down through the Gospels and the Epistles. We leave those rails at our peril. Let us in these days, make sure that we hold onto orthodox Christian belief and practice. Let us make sure that in the essential things of God and Christ, that our "feet" are firmly in His "river-bed" and then we can afford to embrace new and different things. A healthy balance of the Word of God and the Spirit of God will allow you to be creative, original, and even unconventional. You may even become a candidate for the Lord to use you in "strange" ways; where everyone, including yourself might say: "We have all seen "strange things" today!" If your feet are on the ground your head can be in the sky! If you can maintain this posture before God, then all things are possible!

THE GOD OF LEFT FIELD

Every nation seems to have its own set of proverbs, adages, and sayings; and one of the first expressions that I heard here in America was: *"Man, that came out of left field."* This particular phrase (I learned) came out of base-ball terminology where the left fielder has the furthest to throw to first base. So, when the proverbial "ball" comes at you from "left field" it's indicative of something arriving in your life from "out of nowhere" and it has the characteristics of not only being unexpected, but rather odd; rather strange; even a bit weird!

Another base-ball term that I frequently heard was the phrase "curve ball" which basically carries the same thought as "left-field" in that the delivery of a "curve ball" is viewed as a significant deviation from the regular pattern. It's indicative of something coming to you in an unorthodox way that was neither expected nor anticipated.

So, there are times in life when we all experience an event or a situation when out of nowhere, an irregular, significant deviation from the norm is thrown into our lap. And we have to deal with it. This chapter is about this very thing. It's about how to handle yourself when something big; something strange; something out of "left-field" unexpectedly arrives onto the scene of your life.

I have found a man in the Bible from whose life experience we can all learn from; because if *anyone* had something come to him out of "left-field" – if *anyone* had a proverbial "curve-ball" come his way; it had to be Joseph, the adoptive father of Jesus. What happened to him was indeed a significant deviation from the normal or regular pattern. Let's go to the Scriptures and learn from Joseph how to handle events that come from "left-field" and see how after receiving some news that took his breath away; he found his feet and he found his God. To his amazement, he found that God was God even of "left-field."

Matthew 1:18

'Now the birth of Jesus Christ was as follows: After His mother Mary was betrothed to Joseph, before they came together, she was found with child of the Holy Spirit.'

I dare say that there isn't a man alive who hasn't got sympathy for Joseph and his predicament, for if this situation is not "out of left-field" I don't know what is! If this isn't the surprise situation of the centuries, I don't know what is! The girl whom he loved; the one he'd already given himself to in betrothal, - she's pregnant! She is "with child." And furthermore, he's got *nothing* to do with it!

One can only imagine what he must have felt like when he was first told. The news would have hit him hard. This he did *not* expect - not from Mary! He can't believe it of her, and no doubt he would have begun to berate himself for his own lack of wisdom in his choice of her. "I have chosen wrongly and I have chosen badly" he must have thought to himself.

More was to come. If the news of the pregnancy came out of "left-field" then truly the "curve-ball" came when she said that she hadn't been with anyone! That extra information is indeed a significant deviation from the regular pattern! It's got to be the greatest "curve-ball" in history! For Joseph and for *all* men everywhere, his wife's explanation was simply, unbelievable.

When Mary told him the news, he went into "action mode" as most of *us* tend to do. Something big, something unexpected and unanticipated, had just happened to him and the consequences of it all were huge. Like most men in the world when they receive devastating news, Joseph set about trying to fix the problem. Although his marriage to Mary had not been consummated, they were still viewed as husband and wife through their betrothal; and in Jewish life, sexual sins were considered very seriously, especially if committed by a young maiden. Virginity and consequential proofs of virginity were of extreme importance and any aberration of those things was hazardous - to say the least!

Joseph began to gather his thoughts and ponder over what would be the best course of action. Clearly, he could no longer consider having Mary as his life partner and the forth-coming wedding arrangements must be cancelled. Shocked to the core with what Mary had told him, he must have thought: "I need to break off this betrothal. I've got see a lawyer who can be discreet; who can wrap this thing up legally and quietly, so that Mary isn't publicly shamed for what she's done."

Matthew 1:19

'Then Joseph her husband, being a just man, and not wanting to make her a public example, was minded to put her away secretly.'

We can be grateful to Matthew for inserting that sentence in his account because it reveals the normal human reaction to unwelcome events; for the natural response to major difficulties is to try and "make the problem go away."

Granted, there are some incidents in life that require an

immediate response because they have come from a place which demands a prompt reply. For example, a direct challenge to authority must be quickly checked, because order has to be maintained; and there's a difference between defending one's self and defending one's authority. But this situation which has been revealed to us in Joseph's life, is not like that.

These events signify the times when life has put us into a predicament; when something embarrassingly odd has come to us from "out of left-field" - which means that not only is it surprising, it also very perplexing. When something arrives from "left field" it comes loaded with questions. It brings with it a note of bewilderment which causes everyone of us to say: "What just happened there?"

Human reaction says, "Fix the problem" but wisdom says, *"Better tackle the question before you attack the problem."*

And so, you will find in matters like these; when your situations arrive out of "left-field" and when you've been hurt and offended by the unexpected - First Base is *not* "action-stations." First Base is prayerful thought where you can bring it all to God and say, "Lord, what do these things mean?" The next verses find Joseph at *wisdom's* "first base."

Matthew 1: 20-21

'But while he thought about these things, behold an angel of the Lord appeared to him in a dream, saying, "Joseph, son of David, do not be afraid to take to you Mary your wife, for that which is conceived in her is of the Holy Spirit.

And she will bring forth a Son, and you shall call His name Jesus, for He will save His people from their sins."'

These Scriptures tell us how to begin handling any "curve-ball" that arrives suddenly in our lives. When it comes to dealing with something out of "left-field" first-base is this - *"give it some thought."* There were many thoughts flooding Joseph's mind and there were a lot of things that Joseph was ready to do; but *"while he thought on these things"* God began to speak! While Joseph pondered upon the things he had been told, God soon began to "put him in the picture."

We can learn from Joseph in these matters. We can learn that "first base" is to prayerfully think about it all. The *question* of the hour must be addressed *first*. In this case, God gave a full explanation of what was going on. However, in Job's situation, no explanation was given; but whether we receive an answer or not, the *question* must be handled *first*. One way or another it has to be "put to bed" and the only way that can be done successfully is an acknowledgment from us that God is God and that He can do what He wants with His own. Only *then*, when we have recognized that our Heavenly Father is God of the *whole* field of our lives, can we *begin* to think about a course of action. Only *then* can we allow "second base" to come into our sights.

"Whilst he thought on these things" God began to speak!

Oh, that we would all learn this lesson well; to prayerfully respond to God first, rather than to jump into action. As I said, our human inclination is to go into action to get rid of the problem - that is, the problem as we see it. Too many of us adopt a "ready, fire, aim" position when uncomfortable situations spring upon us.

Joseph thought about everything that Mary had said; deliberated over what had just happened to him, and then God responded in a dream, saying, *"Do not be afraid to take to you Mary your wife, for that which is conceived in her is of the Holy Spirit. She is going to bear a Son who will save His people from their sins and you are to call him Jesus."*

Through that revelation, the Lord answered the "question of the hour" for him and from that moment his befuddled mind found a level of understanding, enabling him to then run for Second Base. With his heart at peace, he could then begin to take action. Having understood the "why" of the situation, he could now concentrate on the "what" - the "what to do next" part.

Matthew 1: 24

'Then Joseph, being aroused from sleep, did as the angel of the Lord commanded him and took to him his wife.'

Second Base for Joseph was to be obedient to what he now knew and to put into action all the things necessary to fulfill the will of God. He immediately took Mary back into his loving arms. She had *not* betrayed his love for her, and I dare say that she was now more precious to him than she'd ever been! Joseph now understood that his darling wife was the one chosen to be the mother of his Lord! The secret hope of every maiden in Israel was now a quiet reality in the womb of his wife Mary.

Destiny had come to this couple in a strange yet magnificent way. From the human perspective it had come out of "left-field" but with God, not only are all things possible; they all make sense - at least to His mind.

So, Joseph fully restored his relationship with Mary, but it was on a completely different foundation. A set of new responsibilities towards her and the Child she was carrying came keenly into focus. Having understood the mystery of it all and having taken Mary back into his embrace; a further requirement would now be necessary. It would lead Joseph to the Third Base in the process where after publicly marrying his bride, he deliberately avoided consummating the marriage in a physical way. He disciplined himself in his natural desires to have her, until after the Child - the Holy Child Jesus, had been born.

Matthew 1: 25

'And did not know her till she had brought forth her firstborn Son. And he called His name Jesus.'

Fourth Base is found in this portion of Scripture. Joseph touches the "home-plate" when, having done everything he could to fulfill God's will; he named the Child, Jesus. It was he who gave the Child its name and confirmed its destiny. Well done Joseph!

The whole experience had come to him suddenly and unexpectedly, but after the initial shock, he handled himself very well. It was the most unusual of circumstances, for no man had ever encountered anything remotely like it! But, he thought about things first and discovered that God knows what He's doing and that He is larger than life's events, even the odd, surprising ones.

What we learn from this particular story, is that God is not only bigger than life's events; He is often the One Who's sending them! God doesn't just cope with "left-field" - He commands it! God *owns* "left-field." The *whole* field of life belongs to Him and therefore He can send something into our lives that has no rhyme nor reason - at least to our minds. As it was in the case of Joseph and Mary, when unexpected things happen to us, we can only accept what has taken place and say like the Psalmist: *"This was the Lord's doing; it is marvelous in our eyes!"*

It's quite possible that, like Joseph, you too have just received news from out of "the blue" - from out of "left-field." You never saw it coming. How could you? It came out of nowhere but it's now in your lap. You're thinking of how to fix it. You're ready to make decisions that will solve the problem or at least alleviate the situation. In your heart and mind, you just want to make it go away. The impulse to fire before you aim is strong but please halt and learn from Joseph to tackle the "question of the hour" first! Think deeply about what's happened and take the matter to God whom the prophet Daniel described as the 'Revealer of Secrets.' The 'God of Heaven' knows everything and the answer to the "why" of the situation lies with Him. Seek the Lord for the reasons as to why the events have taken place and let Him help you answer the questions in your mind. If there is no answer or explanation from God then at least be at peace with what the situation suggests; being assured with the knowledge that *all* things have "passed through" His hands before they ever came to you.

Joseph's success in handling his situation began when he decided to first think about it all; and it wasn't long after that when God began to speak to him! Whether God gives you an answer or not, you can be sure of two things. Firstly, you can be assured of His peace no matter how bewildering the situation is. Secondly, there will be a "voice" in it all - even if you can't immediately interpret its message. The Bible tells us that "wisdom is justified in her children." You may not understand what has just happened to you but you will probably understand it later; when the fruit of God's wisdom is seen in its harvest. When Jesus stooped down to wash His disciple's feet, he said to Peter: *"What I am doing, you do not understand now, but you will know after this."*

While God can be clearly understood in many aspects, there remains numerous areas of mystery in connection with His ways. He told us all quite emphatically through the prophet Isaiah, that: *"As the heavens are higher than the earth, so are My ways higher than your ways, and My thoughts than your thoughts."*

So, there are some things that come to us that use the direct approach but as we have discovered in this chapter, there are some things that come to us from seemingly nowhere. They are unexpected, unanticipated and inexplicable. They came out of "left field." But, because God is Who He says He is, He therefore *owns* "left-field." "Left-field" *belongs* to Him and its an area of life that allows Him to work mysteriously and yet wonderfully in our lives. When moments like these visit us, our response should be like that of Mary, when she first heard the astounding news of what was to take place in her life. She said to the angel who spoke to her: *"Let it be unto me according to your word."*

Maybe this kind of life experience is not happening to you right now; but try and remember this word when it does! It will prove to be a "word of wisdom" from the Lord at that time in your life.

BENJAMITES – MEN OF THE LEFT HAND

This chapter will help us to once again observe how God uses that which was not expected. *All* things are at His disposal and therefore He can use *all* things for His glory. The versatility of God in our lives is something to marvel at and the Scriptures reveal just how ambidextrous God can be! He works on the left *and* the right hand.

Job 23: 8-10

"'Look, I go forward, but He is not there, and backward, but I cannot perceive Him; When He works on the left hand, I cannot behold Him; When He turns to the right hand, I cannot see Him. But He knows the way that I take; when He has tested me, I shall come forth as gold.'"

The Scriptures leave us in no doubt that great significance is attached to God's *right* hand. In the Scriptures the phrase "right-hand" occurs one hundred and sixty-six times in which they also speak of our "right-hand" too! For example, in Isaiah, it says: *"For I the Lord God, hold your right hand; it is I who say to you, "Fear not, I am the One who helps you."*

The "right-hand" symbolizes authority and therefore signifies power and strength. Moses equated the right hand of God with His power, attributing the parting of the Red

Sea to the strength of God's right hand. He also spoke of God descending in flaming fire, to write the commandments on tablets of stone with the finger of His right hand. There are many Biblical references of God exalting the Person or the work of His right hand.

King David was shown a revelation of this truth and he testified of it when he said: *"The Lord said unto my lord; Sit at my right hand until I make your enemies your footstool!"* It was a prophetic revelation of the Messiah who would take up His position at the right hand of God. When David saw this scene, it was prophetic in nature but since the resurrection of his Lord, it is now fact! Jesus is now sitting at the right hand of God, being invested by God with all power and authority. Have you ever heard the saying, "He's my right-hand man"? Jesus Christ is God's right-hand Man!

The right hand was also regarded as the "hand of blessing" and this was vividly portrayed for us when Jacob blessed Joseph's two children. The Bible tells us that *'Israel stretched out his right hand and laid it on the head of Ephraim, who was the younger and his left hand on the head of Manasseh, crossing his hands for Manasseh was the first-born.'*

There was also a sacrificial significance to the right side in that Aaron and his sons would have both blood and anointing oil put on their right ear lobes; their right thumbs and their right big toes.

The right side or the right hand of God will figure greatly at the end of this present age. The Bible tells us that *'The Lord will gather all nations and He will separate the people, one from another as a shepherd separates the sheep from the goats; and He will place the sheep on His right, but the goats on the left. Then the King will say to those on His right hand, "Come, you who are blessed of My Father, inherit the kingdom which was prepared for you from the foundation of the world.*

103

For those on the left hand, He will say "Depart from Me, you cursed, into the everlasting fire prepared for the Devil and his angels."

So, you can see by these examples some of the reasons why through the years, the right hand has always been favored over the left. In some cultures, the left-hand is even associated with bad omens. They see the right-hand as being lucky and the left-hand as being unlucky. In Arabic, for example, the word "simal" means both "left-hand' and "bad omen." Even the Latin word for left-handed has a connotation of the word "sinister' and there have been times in the past when school teachers have forced left-handed pupils to write their essays with their *right* hands!

Through the ages then, left-handedness has been seen as odd, undesirable - even anti-social.

However, as Job declared, God *works* on the left hand! While the Scriptures exalt the right-hand they don't denigrate the left! Indeed, there are stories in the Bible of left-handed heroes and interestingly, they all come from a certain tribe in Israel. In this chapter I want us to take a look at the unusual proclivities inherent within them. They were the Benjamites, and they were known as "men of the left-hand." The irony of this statement lies in their very name, because the name "Benjamin" means "son of the right hand."

Genesis 35: 16-18

'Then they journeyed from Bethel. And when there was but a little distance to go to Ephrath, Rachel labored in childbirth, and she had hard labor.

Now it came to pass, when she was in hard labor, that the midwife said to her "Do not fear; you will have this son also."

And so it was, as her soul was departing (for she died),

that she called his name Ben Oni; but his father called him Benjamin.'

In Bible times, the delivery of a new-born child was often viewed through the lens of the prophetic and the child was named accordingly. This baby's birth was extremely painful and difficult, bringing great sorrow to the parents as its delivery took away the life of the mother. As the mother was departing into the next life in great anguish, she gave him the name Ben Oni, which means "the son of my sorrow." But Jacob her husband and father of the child didn't allow that name to continue and renamed him Ben-jamin which means "the son of the right hand." He gave him an illustrious name rather than a name with negative connotations. However, there remained "sorrow" hidden in the prophetic wings of this child for as he grew and became a tribe in Israel, his descendants would bring great sorrow upon the rest of the House of Israel. Only God's grace prevented them from being totally eliminated!

Nevertheless, the Benjamites would play an important role in the life and times of the nation. Though they would be referred to as "little Benjamin" and though they would inherit the smallest territory in the Promised Land; they were destined to perform significant events throughout the history of God's People. Jerusalem, the place where God chose to put His Name was in their territory and they would lead even the princes of Judah in the processions of God into His temple. The first king of Israel came from them and most of our New Testament today can be attributed to a man from the tribe of Benjamin! So, while they have been small, their contribution has been significant.

However, what is of most interest for us to observe is the fact that multitudes of Benjamites were known for their left-handedness. It seems that they were quite an ambidextrous tribe; able to use both right and left hand but with propensities favoring the left. For example, the Benjamites that came to David could use *both* hands for war. However, the Book of Judges tells us that one of the military skill-sets that the men of Benjamin possessed was found in a regiment of their valiant men who could sling stones with their left hand and not miss!

Judges 20: 15-16

'And from their cities at that time the children of Benjamin numbered twenty-six thousand men who drew the sword, beside the inhabitants of Gibeah, who numbered seven hundred select men. Among all this people were seven hundred select men who were left-handed; every one could sling a stone at a hair's breadth and not miss.'

At that time, men from the tribe of Benjamin had committed a great sin against God and against Israel as a people. The nation as a whole had fallen into the seemingly endless cycle of "doing evil in the sight of the Lord" and on this occasion, civil war broke out. The Benjamites were valiant warriors and they and their crack troops proved very difficult to overcome. The Lord however was against them and through the rest of the tribes of Israel, He eventually crushed their resistance, leaving them only six hundred men who had fled into the wilderness.

The Book of Judges shows us what happens when God's voice is ignored and everybody does whatever they like!

In those days, God would choose certain individuals, many of them unlikely, and He would cause them to rescue the nation by doing unusual things in unusual ways. God, it seems, is not limited in His methodology and one of the things He used to bring victory was the "left-handedness" of a Benjamite. After Othniel, the first judge of the nation had died, the nation went "off the tracks" again; and so the Lord disciplined them by strengthening their enemy against them.

Israel's enemy at that time were the Moabites and a man called Eglon was the king of Moab.

(You may remember a former king of Moab called Balak who hired Balaam the prophet to come and curse Israel for him? However, Balaam's curses couldn't prevail at that time because God had *not* found iniquity in Jacob. He had *not* seen wickedness in Israel and consequently, there was *no* sorcery or divination against them. Balaam said to king Balak: *"Look, I have received a command to bless! God has blessed them and I can't reverse it!"*)

Oh, how different things were now.

Judges 3: 12-14

'And the children of Israel again did evil in the sight of the Lord. So the Lord strengthened Eglon, king of Moab against Israel, because they had done evil in the sight of the Lord.

Then he gathered to himself the people of Ammon and Amalek, went and defeated Israel, and took possession of the City of Palms.

So the children of Israel served Eglon, king of Moab eighteen years.'

The enemy defeated Israel and took possession of the City of Palms - which is probably the city of Jericho or a city near that ancient site. For Israel, the disgrace of this defeat at the enemy's hands lay in the alarming fact that they were not just ruling over them administratively, they had now taken up residence *in* the Promised Land! And not only were they *in* the land, they were now stationed at the very "gates" of the nation's original entrance! (He who keeps the doors controls access and egress and "admission prices" are in his power. He can charge whatever he likes to whoever he likes.)

The king of Moab fortified his position in that location

with many soldiers, making the City of Palms a veritable garrison. From there he could command and control the fords of the Jordan river. The enemy was now in the Holy Land and that particular area of the Jordan river belonged to the tribe of Benjamin! The enemy stood on Benjamin's ground, dominating the watery passes of the Jordan River. From there they could control the border crossing and safeguard their access back to the land of Moab if needed. To add insult to injury, the whole House of Israel had to pay tribute to the king of Moab. The situation became intolerable and so the children of Israel began to cry out to the Lord for His help and He chose a man called Ehud, who was a left-handed Benjamite. What happened next was an early version of "mission impossible."

Judges 3:15- 22

'But when the children of Israel cried out to the Lord, the Lord raised up a deliverer for them: Ehud the son of Gera, the Benjamite, a left-handed man. By him the children of Israel sent tribute to Eglon king of Moab.

Now Ehud made himself a dagger (it was double-edged and a cubit in length) and fastened it under his clothes on his right thigh.

So he brought the tribute to Eglon king of Moab. (Now Eglon was a very fat man.) And when he had finished presenting the tribute, he sent away the people who had carried the tribute. But he himself turned back from the stone images that were at Gilgal, and said, "I have a secret message for you O king. He said, "Keep silence!" And all who attended him went out from him.

So Ehud came to him (now he was sitting upstairs in his cool private chamber). Then Ehud said, "I have a message from God for you." So he arose from his seat. Then Ehud reached with his left hand, took the dagger from his right thigh, and thrust it into his belly. Even the hilt went in after the blade, and the fat closed over the blade, for he did not draw the dagger out of his belly; and his entrails came out.'

If there are such things as "minor" miracles, this story has them! Firstly, Ehud was in a position to accomplish all this. *He* was the one chosen to present the tribute to the king of Moab. It was the providential hand of God that had put *him* in charge of the tribute team.

Secondly, he was given the wisdom of secrecy. He made the dagger *himself* and being a naturally left-handed man, (which was unusual) he was able to fasten it under his clothes on his right thigh - a place that no one would expect a weapon to be drawn from.

Thirdly, when he returned to the court of the king of Moab, it was a minor miracle that allowed him to gain such *access* to the king's private chamber and be *alone* with him!

Fourthly, when Ehud saw the overweight king sitting down, he had the presence of mind to say that he had a message from God for him; knowing that he would stand up to receive it, and unwittingly open up the target area for him to stab him in the belly. (God's providential miracles would keep on coming as the events unfolded that day. Ehud would experience God's help in everything he did and by his hand - his left hand, victory would be won.)

Judges 3: 23-30

'Then Ehud went out through the porch and shut the doors of the upper room behind him and locked them. When he had gone out, Eglon's servants came to look, and to their surprise, the doors of the upper room were locked. So they said, "He is probably attending to his needs in the cool chamber."

So they waited till they were embarrassed, and still he had not opened the doors of the upper room. Therefore they took the key and opened them. And there was their master, fallen dead on the floor.

But Ehud had escaped while they delayed, and passed beyond the stone images and escaped to Seirah. And it happened, when he arrived, that he blew the trumpet in the mountains of Ephraim, and the children of Israel went down with him from the mountains; and he led them.

Then he said to them, "Follow me, for the Lord has delivered your enemies the Moabites into your hand." So they went down after him, seized the fords of the Jordan leading to Moab, and did not allow anyone to cross over.

At that time they killed about ten thousand men of Moab, all stout men of valor; not a man escaped.

So Moab was subdued that day under the hand of Israel. And the land had rest for eighty years.'

Ehud experienced a fifth minor miracle when having stabbed the king of Moab to death there was no commotion heard by the king's servants. This allowed Ehud to quietly close the doors and make his way out. Another providential miracle was that the king was in his private chamber when all this took place. That fact alone gave Ehud those vital minutes that he needed for his escape, for the servants were reluctant to disturb the king unnecessarily. Their delay in opening the doors was just what Ehud needed to make his way out of the palace. By the time the alarm was sounded, he was well on his way home.

Sixthly, a minor miracle took place when Ehud blew the war trumpet in the mountains of Ephraim and the men of Israel rallied to him. They believed his story about his slaying of the king of Moab and moreover, they were willing to go and fight the Moabites with him! After eighteen years of oppression, they were ready to follow a man who had the "hand of God" upon his life.

Ehud led them down to the fords of Jordan and there they isolated the men of Moab from their own country, denying them access across the river. By the end of the day, there wasn't one Moabite left in the Promised Land. There wasn't one Moabite standing on the inheritance of Benjamin.

God works on the left-hand! He used Ehud, the left-handed Benjamite to surprise and slay the enemy. Once again, God used a *man* and a *method* that wasn't expected. The king of Moab didn't know what had hit him! It came to him, as it were, out of "left-field." As we have noted in the previous chapter of this book, God owns left-field! He delights in using unlikely people to do unexpected things!

Oh, little Benjamin! Oh, left-handed Benjamin! Oh, the things that God can do with that which is small and with that which is unusual. The Lord delights in placing His power upon unlikely people who then use unusual methods. The Scriptures contain *many* examples of these things. They tell us of the ox goad of Shamgar; the trumpets and lanterns of Gideon; the jaw-bone of a donkey in Samson's hand and the sling and stone in David's.

We're never too small for God to use us. We may feel like "little Benjamin" but the Lord can give us some unusual abilities in which we become so skillful in their use; that like the left-handed men of Benjamin, we cannot miss!

THE JUXTAPOSITIONS OF GOD

Juxtaposition! What is a juxtaposition? 'Juxtaposition' is a literary term that means to place unrelated, contrary, concepts side by side for contrast, irony and surprisingly, for unity! When an author brings two contrasting thoughts together, he or she uses the juxtaposition to highlight their opposing and yet their combined unified meaning.

When Charles Dickens wrote the book 'A tale of two cities' he began his famous work with this juxtaposition: *"It was the best of times; it was the worst of times."*

William Shakespeare used the concept of juxtaposition as his two starry-eyed lovers, Romeo and Juliet found love in each other; despite the fact that they both came from opposing families.

In Brazil, they combine a white cheese with a red jam/jelly and they call it "Romeo and Juliet." (I was offered this dish many times but I couldn't get past the optics of the contrast. I would say, "No thanks, there's just something odd about that combination that doesn't sit well with me." I thought that I had a case until they said to me. "You eat cheesecake, don't you?")

These are just some examples of juxtaposition in words, concepts and food, but there are far greater juxtapositions than these.

They are the *great* juxtapositions of God!

In the beginning, God created us male and female. If ever there were contrasting and yet combining elements placed together, it was right there and then! What do people say? "Men are from Mars and women are from Venus." Indeed, sometimes it *is* hard to understand each other. We're the same in so many ways and yet very different in many other aspects, but God has put us together. In His wisdom, He joined us, and *together* we bring forth the sweetness of love into the world; and at the same time, this God-ordained union provides humanity's "building blocks" through what we produce together - the wonderful family unit.

In the skies, God created great lights. He created the sun to rule the day and the moon to rule the night. The sun and the moon are very different entities. The sun is much larger than the moon and it has its own internal lighting system whereas the moon has no light of its own. But when God put them together; when He placed the sun and the moon in orbital juxtaposition, this wonderful combination was able to govern the whole planet with their lights and their pulse; marking off times and seasons for those living on the earth.

Even more essential than the constellations are the two elements of gas that God has made for life to exist. The life force of the earth is water - good old H_2O - in which God has joined two parts of hydrogen to one-part of oxygen. Where would be without *that* natural juxtaposition? It is indeed a creative arrangement of God.

So, God takes things that are different; even contrasting, and He brings them together. He causes them to exist side by side and in that partnership, they serve an even greater purpose than if they'd remained alone.

One of the most precious stories in the Bible is the story of Ruth and her mother-in-law Naomi. Their lives together were an arrangement of God and they were a juxtaposition in themselves. The story of their relationship went something like this: Hard times had come upon the people of God for there was a famine in the land. In Bethlehem, there was a man called Elimelech who had a wife and two sons. His wife's name was Naomi. Because the famine was so severe, they decided to leave their country and go into the land of Moab. While they were there, Elimelech the father died and Naomi was left with her two sons. The two sons married two women from Moab. One woman was called Orpah and the other was called Ruth. They all lived together in the land of Moab for about ten years. Then, tragically, the two sons died, leaving Naomi bereft and so she decided to return to her country where her relatives were still living. She'd also heard that better times had come to those in her home town of Bethlehem and so she set off for home. Her daughters in law loved her dearly and they accompanied her on her journey, but Naomi released them both to go back home to their families. Reluctantly, Orpah did so, but Ruth refused and clung to her mother-in-law.

Ruth 1: 14-19

'Then they lifted up their voices and wept again; and Orpah kissed her mother-in-law, but Ruth clung to her. And she said, "Look, your sister-in-law has gone back to her people and to her gods; return after your sister-in-law."

But Ruth said: "Entreat me not to leave you, or to turn back from you; for wherever you go, I will go; and wherever you lodge, I will lodge; Your people shall be my people, and your God, my God.

Where you die, I will die, and there I will be buried. The Lord do so to me, and more also, if anything but death parts you and me."

When she saw that she was determined to go with her, she stopped speaking to her.

Now the two of them went until they came to Bethlehem.

And it happened, when they had come to Bethlehem, that all the city was excited because of them; and the women said, "Is this Naomi?"'

This scene with Ruth and her Jewish mother-in-law is full of juxtaposition; for Ruth was a Moabite, of whom Israel in general, had no dealings with. As the two of them began to make their way to Bethlehem, they made a very unlikely pair indeed!

"An odd couple" - as they say!

Here in this story, we see that there are two things happening at the same time. One aspect is visible and the other is invisible.

In the visible aspect, we see the wonderful heart of Ruth; how she loved Naomi and how she clung to her; beseeching her *not* to send her away. The words that Ruth said to Naomi at that time are as precious today as when they were first spoken.

"Where you go, I will go. Where you stay, I will stay. Your people shall be my people and your God shall be my God. Where you die, there will I also be buried."

The *invisible* aspect of this moment was the "hand of God" in it all because He was bringing this relationship into juxtaposition for His more wider and deeper purposes in the world. God had *eternal* plans going on that both of them wouldn't be able to see at that time. This juxtaposition of two different women from two cultural backgrounds was an arrangement of God.

There are some people that the Lord brings into *our* lives who are easy to connect with. There's nothing quite like working with like-minded people who have the same disposition as one's self.

However, not all of God's combinations are "like for like." This story of Ruth and her mother-in-law tells us that on some occasions, God puts opposites together. Sometimes He puts people with contrasting elements side by side to where even friction can easily build up between them. In His wisdom, God often puts contrary natured characters together so that they both learn another side of things. He calls them to work together and through His grace, they learn to appreciate each other's qualities and at the same time, they learn how to forgive much!

God has arranged that juxtaposition in their lives for His glory.

The Bible tells us that Christ is the Vine and that we are the branches. Have you noticed that grapes come in clusters? They don't harvest one grape at a time. They harvest grapes in bunches. What does that mean to us both spiritually and practically? It means that while we can retain and even celebrate our individuality, our *overall* fruitfulness is going to hang on who we've been *linked* with! Wouldn't it be nice if we liked everyone we have been linked with? Wouldn't it be nice if we got on well with the whole bunch? In His wisdom, God sometimes puts us with "grapes" that we *don't* like! He asks us to join people who "rub us up the wrong way" and with folks that aren't easy to be around. Sometimes, He puts us with people that we find hard to relate to, and their close proximity brings an uncomfortable pressure. Yes, grapes bring pressure to each other! The weight of a fully developed cluster can squeeze the life out of the grapes on its particular branch.

How many times have we withdrawn ourselves from someone simply because we felt that we didn't connect? How many times have we refused to work alongside someone simply because we didn't like them? God understands that our human nature has a propensity to associate with that which is most comfortable, but when God wants to change your character to be more like His, there are people who you are just destined to meet! The Lord is a genius at putting people together and His invisible hand governs who comes into our lives. If we try to avoid certain people, the Lord will often bring situations into our lives where we will find ourselves cornered either by those very people or with somebody exactly like them! Be prepared for situations like that. They are the arrangements of God. They are the juxtapositions of God and they are unavoidable!

If we can be at peace with whomever God decides to bring into our lives, we will have won the greatest of victories - the victory over self! However, this principle of association doesn't stop at juxtaposition. To be placed *side by side* is one thing but to be placed *inside* is quite another! This placing *inside* is called "grafting."

What exactly is "grafting"? Grafting is the word that describes the joining of one thing *into* another. There is a reason why we graft and there is method as to how we do it. The reason why we graft two different plants together is so that we can enjoy the benefits of them *both*. A successful graft will bring forth greater growth and better fruit. It's the joining of their *differences* that cause the plant to flourish. When nature is confined to "sameness" it can suffer weakness. One of the reasons why they cross-breed dogs is to eliminate some of their inherent weaknesses and the result is referred to as "the vigor of the mixed breed."

Many years ago, my supervisor at work told me about his trip to Canada, where he had heard folks speak of a remote village in which the people living there were gradually going blind. Apparently, the community still wore all the old tartan of their ancestry. Down through the many years, they had largely remained in their location and consequently, their marriages were all "in-house." No other "elements" had come into their reproductive systems and weaknesses became inherent.

So, grafting produces healthy, vigorous growth and that's why farmers do it.

How is "grafting" done? The tree-surgeon will first find a quality old root-stock from which he can then graft a younger plant into. He cuts into the old root-stock; making an upside-down T- cut, right where the bud growth is. This is actually painful for the plant because it really is surgery. The Greek word for stylus is "graphein" which is a "cutting" by etching or by writing. The younger plant that is to be grafted *in* is cut down to a small piece and has all its leaves stripped away. It is then inserted *into* the cut that has been made in the main root. The two plants are then bound tightly together, with the smaller, young plant, inside the larger, older one. At that point, the only thing showing on the outside is the bud of the younger plant now sitting on the nub of the old one. The older plant then begins to feed the younger plant through the bud and the new growth that comes is always greater and the fruit that follows is always better. As the Scriptures say, *"Two are better than one for they have a good reward for their labor."*

This is what God had planned for Ruth all along. Her life was initially placed in *juxtaposition* with Naomi; but when Boaz came along and married Ruth, she was *grafted* in to the Olive Tree of Abraham, Isaac and Jacob. Through her marital union with Boaz, Ruth the Moabite was brought in to the "Israel of God." And look at the fruit of that graft! Ruth and Boaz had a son and his name was Obed. Obed was the father of Jesse; who was the father of David - king David!

Oh, the mysteries of the juxtapositions and the grafting's of God!

Has this not also happened to us? Have we not as Gentiles been grafted into the Vine; into Christ? Yes, we have! He is from the stock of Abraham. He *is* the Root and Offspring of David and at Calvary's Cross, He was cut for us. The stylus of

God's pen wrote our names in the palms of His hands and we were grafted into a new covenant! Hallelujah, what a Savior!

And was there ever an opposing situation greater than the gulf between Jew and Gentile? There was a "wall" between us both but through the cutting of Christ on the Cross, Jesus broke down that "middle wall of partition" and joined the two peoples into one unified Body! The enmity that had previously been there was totally eradicated and His blood offering has given us all peace with God and with each other!

Romans 11: 16- 24

'For if the firstfruit is holy, the lump is also holy; and if the root is holy, so are the branches. And if some of the branches were broken off, and you, being a wild olive tree, were grafted in among them, and with them became a partaker of the root and fatness of the olive tree, do not boast against the branches. But if you do boast, remember that you do not support the root, but the root supports you.

You will say then, "Branches were broken off that I might be grafted in." Well said. Because of unbelief they were broken off, and you stand by faith. Do not be haughty, but fear. For if God did not spare the natural branches, He may not spare you either.

Therefore consider the goodness and severity of God; on those who fell, severity; but toward you, goodness, if you continue in His goodness. Otherwise you also will be cut off. And they also, if they do not continue in unbelief, will be grafted in, for God is able to graft them in again.

For if you were cut out of the olive tree which is wild by nature, and were grafted contrary to nature into a cultivated olive tree, how much more will these, who are natural branches be grafted into their own olive tree?'

These Scriptures figure very highly in my life because at the time of writing this book, I am the senior pastor of a church that meets in a Jewish synagogue! As a congregation, we are living this juxtaposition of God. He has placed us alongside a large Jewish community in the city in which we live. The irony of the situation is that in Christ, we are more grafted in to the "Israel of God" than they are! They are Abraham's children according to the flesh but we are Abraham's children according to the promise in Christ! We have atonement for our sins - they do not. We have the gift of eternal life - they do not. However, we are there alongside them, being placed in their temple by God for His purposes. It is an arrangement of God. It is a juxtaposition of God. And we pray that one day, many of them will turn to their Messiah, and by so doing, we can all be grafted into the "Olive Tree" together.

The challenge that comes to us all in these truths is that it allows the Lord to ask everyone the question: "How much can I use you?" Experienced Christians will tell us that to be used by God will require from us a deep knowledge of His grace, for it is His grace that enables us to love people - even the difficult ones! We all find it easy to love God, but it's quite another thing to love God's people.

The "bottom line" is this: God is in the business of bringing people together for life and for ministry. For some, *side by side* may be close enough. That "juxtaposition" might be sufficient for where you want to be. But what if God wants to take you deeper and *join* you into a person's life and ministry? Does He want to "graft" you in? If this is what God wants; be assured that He is not seeking to put a control mechanism onto your life, but rather to produce a growth factor that you haven't previously known. He desires that in the combining of lives - however dissimilar; that the "tree" of each one will know greater growth and better fruit!

As you are approaching the end of this chapter, there are some questions that you can now ask the Lord, like: "Lord, what is Your arrangement for me at this time? Is what I'm experiencing a seasonal juxtaposition or is it a more permanent graft?"

You will find that there is mutual benefit in the "juxtaposition" but there is blessing and eternal purpose in the "graft." Allow the Lord to accomplish both in your life - through "the best of times and the worst of times."

To Provide or not to Provide

One of William Shakespeare's most famous lines is 'To be or not to be? - that is the question.' In this chapter on the unusual ways of God, I'd like to write a line of my own in a similar fashion and it is: 'To provide or not to provide - that is the question.'

As I read through the Word of God, I find that there are times when "to make provision" is right and "to make no provision" is wrong. I also find that there are times when "to make provision" in certain situations is wrong and "to make no provision" is right! Obviously, the answer to the question of whether to provide or not to provide, lies in the character and in the context of the situation.

Let's take a look at some situations in which to make provision was right and to have made no provision would have been wrong - or at the very least, negligent.

The first example that comes to mind is that of Noah. God told Noah what was coming to the world and He told him to make provision for his family by building a boat.

Genesis 6: 13-19

'And God said to Noah, "The end of all flesh has come before Me, for the earth is filled with violence through them; and behold, I will destroy them with the earth.

Make yourself an ark of gopherwood; make rooms in the ark and cover it inside and outside with pitch.

And this is how you shall make it: The length of the ark shall be three hundred cubits, its width fifty cubits, and its height thirty cubits. You shall make a window for the ark, and you shall finish it to a cubit from above; and set the door of the ark in its side. You shall make it with lower, second and third decks.

And behold I Myself am bringing floodwaters on the earth, to destroy from under heaven all flesh in which is the breath of life; everything that is on the earth shall die.

But I will establish My covenant with you; and you shall go into the ark - you, your sons, your wife and your sons' wives with you. And of every living thing of all flesh you shall bring two of every sort into the ark, to keep them alive with you; they shall be male and female.

The Bible confirms Noah's obedience when it said: *"Thus Noah did; according to all that God commanded him, so he did."* God commanded him to make provision for his family and for all of God's creatures and thank God he did, for none of us would be here if he hadn't! The wonderful truth that's hidden in the story of Noah is that in building the ark, Noah made provision for *us!*

There are many more examples of God commanding or leading His servants to provide things for His people. He commanded Moses to provide quality men to become judges in the nation. He allowed David to make provision for his son Solomon, so that he would have everything he would need to build the Temple of God in Jerusalem. Throughout the Scriptures we see confirmation of the general principle of making provision for our families. The Book of Proverbs says: *"A good man leaves an inheritance to his children's children."* Providing for the family's future is one of the responsibilities of all men of God.

This is something the New Testament totally agrees with

and it is endorsed by the apostle Paul in one of his letters to his son in the faith -Timothy.

1 Timothy 5: 8

'But if anyone does not provide for his own, and especially for those of his household, he has denied the faith and is worse than an unbeliever.'

Clearly, providing for yourself and for your family is a Godly thing to do. It shows that you have been faithful in your duties and in your obligations towards them. Making provision is a good and healthy thing to do, especially if it includes meeting the future needs of *others*. When it is only about one's self, it loses its altruism and runs the risk of missing God's blessing.

Luke 12: 15-21

'And He said to them, "Take heed and beware of covetousness, for one's life does not consist in the abundance of the things he possesses." Then He spoke a parable to them, saying: "The ground of a certain rich man yielded plentifully. And he thought within himself, saying 'What shall I do, since I have no room to store my crops?'

"So he said, 'I will do this: I will pull down my barns and build greater, and there I will store all my crops and my goods. And I will say to my soul, "Soul, you have many goods laid up for many years; take your ease; eat, drink and be merry."'

"But God said to him, 'Fool! This night your soul will be required of you; then whose will those things be which you have provided?' So is he who lays up treasure for himself, and is not rich toward God."

The key to understanding this kind of selfish provision is found in the Lord's preamble to the parable itself. He was warning his listeners to take heed and beware of covetousness. The rich man in the parable was laying up treasure for himself. So good, healthy provision largely depends upon the inward motives of the heart. The focus has to be on the "why" and not on the "what" or the "how." On the other hand, those whose focus is on the Lord and on *His* Kingdom will not only be enabled to make provision for others; they will also experience the effortless provision of God for *themselves!*

Luke 12: 22-24

'Then He said to His disciples, "Therefore I say to you, do not worry about your life, what you will eat; nor about the body, what you will put on. Life is more than food and the body is more than clothing.

Consider the ravens, for they neither sow nor reap, which have neither storehouse nor barn; and God feeds them. Of how much more value are you than the birds?"'

Jesus went on to talk about the lilies and how they grow in effortless profusion and how the grass of the field is clothed by God. *"How much more will He clothe you, O you of little faith?"* Jesus said.

Let us now take a look at the other side of the "coin" and find examples in the Bible when "not to provide" is the right thing to do - and yes, this aspect can be more difficult to achieve.

First of all, the apostle Paul tells us in Romans to put on the Lord Jesus Christ and make "no provision" for the flesh to fulfill its lusts. The same portion of Scripture tells us to put on the armor of light and cast off the works of darkness.

In other words: *"Don't stray off the path! Don't drift away into the darkness of this world. There are "monsters" out there and they will eat you alive! Make "no provision" for them! Watch where you're going! Don't close your eyes and fall asleep. Awake to righteousness and keep your eyes on Jesus and His Word!"*

The apostle Peter was a man known for being a bit "up and down" in his character but he became a "rock" on which the 'Early Church' believers put their confidence in. Peter found a path to consistency, even to the point where he was assured that he would never let the Lord down again; like he had done on that dreadful night of denial.

2 Peter 1: 5-11

'But also for this very reason, giving all diligence, add to your faith virtue, to virtue knowledge, to knowledge self-control, to self-control perseverance, to perseverance godliness, to godliness brotherly kindness and to brotherly kindness love.

For if these things are yours and abound, you will be neither barren nor unfruitful in the knowledge of our Lord Jesus Christ. For he who lacks these things is short-sighted, even to blindness, and has forgotten that he was cleansed from his old sins.

Therefore, brethren, be even more diligent to make your call and election sure, for if you do these things you will never stumble; for so an entrance will be supplied to you abundantly into the everlasting kingdom of our Lord and Savior Jesus Christ.'

The apostle Peter is telling us that if we continue to inculcate this kind of Godly provision into our lives we will *never* stumble! By making no provision for the flesh to fulfill its lusts and by making provision for the soul to fulfill its destiny, we see the two sides of the one "coin."

Another example of when "not to provide" is when you

have acknowledged that God is in charge of something and therefore you only have stewardship in it. As a Minister for many years, I have officiated at many "dedication services" where businesses, ministries, homes, etc., have all been officially placed into God's hands. The prayers that have been prayed in those moments have all been heart-felt and sincere, and they have all tended to go something like this: *"Lord, we dedicate this business, this ministry, this home, this whatever, to You. We put it into Your hands this day for we know that this is Your will. It ultimately belongs to You and we believe that You will provide for it; for where You guide - there You provide."*

There is absolutely nothing wrong with prayers of that nature - as long as they stick! Those kinds of prayers are "positional prayers" whereby the Lord is officially given the reins and the preeminence over the whole venture. If we believe that the Lord initiated the vision and that on 'Dedication Day' we began everything in the Holy Spirit; it means that while we must continue to do our part, the vision is ultimately in God's hands! That means - it's not in ours! That means - if it looks like it's going to fail, our appeal is to God and *His* treasury and not ours!

Everybody seems to agree with this in principle, especially on 'Dedication Day' but if or when things take a turn for the worse, causing the situation to appear dire; it's amazing what folks will do to keep everything going! Crisis always comes to that which God initiates because everything He does in our lives must go through its own "death and resurrection." Most Christians are not aware of this, so when a crisis comes to threaten the vision's very existence, they usually respond like people who have no God on their side. Instead of allowing the vision or the enterprise to freefall in God - even to die if necessary; I find even mature believers "pulling out all the stops" to provide for it themselves! Many of them go running to their bank managers for extra loans and some re-mortgage their homes; all with one goal in mind – the rescue of the ministry or the business at hand. *They* make provision for the vision. But if God started it, they are making provision for *God's* vision! God can't allow that and unfortunately, they don't "wake up" until there's absolutely no money left or no way forward. If God owns the enterprise, *He* must decide whether it lives or dies. *He's* the Owner!

This principle is profoundly revealed to us in the life of Abraham who was given a child through a promise made to him by God. After many years of waiting, to the point when it was naturally impossible; the God of the supernatural stepped into Abraham's life, and Isaac was born. It was the Lord who initiated the vision for Abraham to have a son with his wife Sarah in their old age.

One would think that having God in the "business" of it all, that success would come without interruption, but everything that God does knows its own "altar" experience.

Genesis 22: 2-3

'Then He said, "Take now your son, your only son Isaac, whom you love, and go to the land of Moriah, and offer him there as a burnt offering on one of the mountains of which I will tell you."

So Abraham rose early in the morning and saddled his donkey, and took two of his young men with him, and Isaac his son; and he split the wood for the burnt offering, and arose and went to the place of which God had told him.'

This situation was a crisis indeed. He could face it in two ways. He could walk the path of an ordinary man and question the motive and wisdom of God or he could "climb the ladder of faith" and trust God through the whole ordeal. The point of the story is that when God commanded that Isaac should be put to death, Abraham didn't run away from God and try and keep his son alive. His obedience to God would not allow him to "make provision" for what was ultimately *God's* vision.

He made the right choice and he found that God had indeed made provision for His own vision in that He provided a ram to be offered that day instead of Isaac.

If what you are carrying is an "Isaac" then God Himself will provide the lamb! Your "child" will not die! Your business will not fold! Your ministry will not fail! Resist the temptation to take back ownership to try and keep it alive. If you do, you will discover that the "wind" is against you and in the end, you will be defeated and exhausted. If you began in the Spirit, then carry on in it!

Another aspect of this principle of whether to provide or not to provide is found in the realm of personal giving. As Christians, we are all called to serve the poor and needy and financial assistance in most cases is warranted. However, there are many who appear to be in great need but aren't!

When I worked in the poor countries of Eastern Europe, I soon discovered that many gifts of money had been put into the wrong hands. Some of the recipients looked as if they had nothing but we later learned that they had homes of their own. I soon came to learn the Scripture in Isaiah that says, *"with righteousness, the Lord will judge the poor."* Everyone, rich or poor, must be weighed in the scales of God's justice.

Finally, there is the delicate arena of giving to one's acquaintance, friend or family member. There are times when it is one's duty to give and there are times when one must first "hear from the Lord." For many of us, it takes awhile to learn that a *need* is not necessary a *call*. A personal need *can* be a genuine call for help but it's not always a call that we should answer. Sometimes, the correct course of action is "not to provide" because God is doing something in their lives and if your financial assistance is given, you may be frustrating the grace of God working in their lives.

Sometimes, by giving, you are circumventing their spiritual education and you will end up making the situation worse, because they will continue to do what they've always done, and no lessons will have been learned.

"To provide or not to provide" - not always an easy question to answer!

GOLIATH'S SWORD

The contents of this final chapter have been written to serve as a reminder that personal victories won in the past can still prove relevant in the present. Things won many years ago in secret can suddenly be brought out into the glare of a new day; turning that which has been viewed as a *past trophy* into a *present-day tool* - a *tool* for you to use. Such is the story surrounding Goliath's sword. As David said, concerning this weapon – *"There is none like it!"* Let's go to the Scriptures and visit the portion of text that introduces us to this magnificent sword.

1 Samuel 17: 4-11

'And a champion went out from the camp of the Philistines, named Goliath, from Gath, whose height was six cubits and a span. He had a bronze helmet on his head, and he was armed with a coat of mail, and the weight of the coat was five thousand shekels of bronze.

And he had bronze armor on his legs and a bronze javelin between his shoulders. Now the staff of his spear was like a weaver's beam, and his iron spearhead weighed six hundred shekels; and a shield-bearer went before him.

Then he stood and cried out to the armies of Israel, and said to them, "Why have you come out to line up for battle? Am I not a Philistine, and you the servants of Saul? Choose a man for yourselves, and let him come down to me. If he is able

to fight with me and kill me, then we will be your servants.
But if I prevail against him, then you shall be our servants and
serve us."

And the Philistine said, "I defy the armies of Israel this day;
give me a man, that we may fight together."

When Saul and all Israel heard these words of the Philistine,
they were dismayed and greatly afraid.'

What a formidable threat this giant of a man was! He was a
war-machine all on his own! Bronze helmet; coat of iron mail;
bronze shin guards; a bronze javelin at his back; a spear as long
as a weaver's beam complete with a sharp, iron spear-head; a
huge sword at his side and a man to go before him, to carry his
shield! Added to all that, he had a big mouth! His booming
words sent shivers down the spines of all the armies of Israel.
Every day, for forty days, morning and evening, he would step
out of the Philistine ranks to loudly defy God and His people.

"Give me a man that we may fight together!" he cried out.

1 Samuel 17: 24-26

'And all the men of Israel, when they saw the man, fled
from him and were dreadfully afraid. So the men of Israel said,
"Have you seen this man who has come up? Surely he has come
up to defy Israel; and it shall be that the man who kills him, the
king will enrich with great riches, will give him his daughter,
and give his father's house exemption from taxes in Israel."

Then David spoke to the men who stood by him saying,
"What shall be done for the man who kills this Philistine
and takes away the reproach from Israel? For who is this
uncircumcised Philistine that he should defy the armies of the
living God?"'

Here is the first clue as to how young David was viewing
this situation. For David, this wasn't about men against men,

Philistine against Israelite or country against country. He saw this for what it really was. He saw this as a spiritual thing, where this man, this giant of a man, was defying the Living God and all of His armies. This champion of the Philistines had brought a reproach upon Israel and so this situation needed to be seen as a spiritual thing first. I believe that the main purpose of the proceedings that day can be found in the verbal exchanges that went back and forth between David and Goliath as the duel commenced.

1 Samuel 17: 44-47

'And the Philistine said to David, "Come to me, and I will give your flesh to the birds of the air and the beasts of the field!" Then David said to the Philistine, "You come to me with a sword, with a spear, and with a javelin. But I come to you in the name of the Lord of hosts, the God of the armies of Israel, whom you have defied.

This day the Lord will deliver you into my hand, and I will strike you and take your head from you. And this day I will give the carcasses of the camp of the Philistines to the birds of the air and the wild beasts of the earth, that all the earth may know that there is a God in Israel. Then all this assembly shall know that the Lord does not save with sword and spear; for the battle is the Lord's, and He will give you into our hands."

That's what this was all about! "That all the earth may know that there is a God in Israel." This young man David, is full of the Holy Spirit and you really do have to wonder who the real giant is here! Goliath spoke of what he intended to do with David, but David declared what he was going to do not just to Goliath, but to the whole Philistine army! Goliath boasted in his fighting abilities and trusted in his weapons but God had a surprise for him that day. As the Bible says, "Let *not the strong man glory in his strength, nor the armed man in his armor."*

David was effectively saying that Goliath was going to perish that day so that soldiers on *all* sides will know afresh that the Lord doesn't save by sword or by spear, for the battle is the Lord's. The battle is *His* to give, and on this occasion, He gave the victory to David and to the armies of Israel. "He will *give* you into our hands!" David proclaimed.

David ran up the hill towards him and slung a stone towards Goliath's head - and bang! The stone hit him so hard that it sank into his forehead. It made a crater in his skull, causing him to fall head-long to the ground. He was as good as done and David ran to where he was and stood over him! David must have had the same feeling that he experienced in the past when he had slain a lion and a bear which had threatened his father's flock. There is little doubt that the attitude of David that day was predicated upon his past victories; over enemies stronger than him. Little wonder then, that we should feel the boldness of young David when he said to the men of Israel, *"Who is this uncircumcised Philistine that he should defy the armies of the Living God?"* Yes, for David, this was just another day at work!

He didn't have a sword of his own so he got down and drew Goliath's sword out of its sheath and "took care of business" - as they now say. He took care of *God's* business! When the Philistines saw what had happened to their champion, they panicked and ran for home. On the other side of the valley, the Israelites became emboldened and the men of Judah began to shout their war-cry. The God of Israel had just revealed His power and authority and they all witnessed it. With the "voice of Judah" now ringing out, the armies of Israel ran down into the valley; and they pursued the Philistines all the way home.

When they returned from the pursuit they plundered the tents of the Philistine army.

1 Samuel 17: 53-54

'Then the children of Israel returned from chasing the Philistines, and they plundered their tents. And David took the head of the Philistine and brought it to Jerusalem, but he put his armor in his tent.'

David put the spoils of war that he had won into his tent but he brought the head of Goliath - the trophy of the day - to Jerusalem. While many of the children of Israel would have access to Jerusalem, the city was still under the authority of the Jebusites at that time. Nevertheless, it was destined to become the City of David! Whether he knew it or not, David "sowed" the main trophy of his victory that day into his future; that from Jerusalem, he would eventually reign as king over all Israel. As was noted at the beginning of this chapter, this message is a reminder to us that victories won in the past can still be relevant today. They can still find expression in the arena of the present.

David could put all the armor and weapons of Goliath in his own tent because through God's grace, he had legitimately won them! The "tent" doesn't just speak of a place to put them. The "tent" speaks of ownership; of *rightful* ownership. Goliath's weapons of war were now rightfully his! They now *belonged* to David and he put them in *his* tent.

However, it seems that David truly acknowledged that *God* had delivered Goliath into his hands that day; and it looks like David had dedicated most, if not all of those trophies, back to the Lord. This must have been the case because the next time we hear of Goliath's sword, it had been in the possession of the priests at Nob for some time. The sword therefore, was given by David to the house of God as a trophy of God's deliverance!

Such then is the heart of young David. He had the right to keep what he had so bravely won. It was within his power to keep them all, as personal trophies in his own house, but he obviously decided to give God the glory; and so he gave the sword of Goliath to the priests at Nob.

Life moved on quickly for David after that, and little did he know that one day, the trophy of Goliath's sword would once again, become a tool in his hand! David became a great leader in Israel and a favorite of king Saul and his family until fears and petty jealousies in the heart of king Saul ruined everything. David became the king's son-in-law and that close proximity proved to be a dangerous environment for him. Saul became his enemy and on occasions, sought to kill him. Things between them soured to the point where David had to run for his life! The question was: "Where could he run to?" The first place a fugitive in Israel would run to would be the house of God, wherein he could find sanctuary among the priests. He would run to where the Ministers of God could at least help him, if not offer him some degree of protection.

So, David ran to the city called Nob where the priests of the Lord were stationed. They had relocated and brought to Nob what remained of the Tabernacle that had been at Shiloh. They didn't have the ark with them, for the Lord had taken away His glory from the house of Eli; but it seems that they had the rest of the holy furniture necessary to perform their priestly duties. David and the few men that were with him were hungry and so they were given bread from off the holy table. He didn't tell the priests the real story as to why he was there and why he was without weapons. Maybe he tried to keep them in the dark for their own good? David knew the hostility that now surrounded his life and he would have known that when accusations would eventually be hurled, a "cloak of ignorance" for the priests could possibly plead for their innocence. He could see that the chief priest was troubled at his presence there, so he "trod" carefully for himself and for the young men that were with him.

1 Samuel 21: 8-9

'And David said to Ahimelech, "Is there not here on hand a spear or a sword? For I have brought neither my sword nor my weapons with me, because the king's business required haste."

So the priest said, "The sword of Goliath the Philistine, whom you killed in the Valley of Elah, there it is, wrapped in a cloth behind the ephod. If you will take that, take it; for there is no other except that one here."

And David said, "There is none like it; give it to me."'

The priests had no weapons, but there was one sword in the house of the Lord. Hidden behind the ephod and concealed in a cloth, lay the greatest spiritual trophy of the day!

"The sword of Goliath the Philistine, whom you killed in the Valley of Elah, there it is –if you want it." David said to the priest, *"There's none like it; give it to me."*

David took it, and it can be safely presumed that he was then of such a physical stature to where he could now wear and wield such a sword! Clearly, David having earlier offered the sword of Goliath to the house of God; the Lord had kept it for him under wraps, for such a time as this in his life. The sword of Goliath was once rightfully his and having given it to the priests of the Lord, God was now giving it back to him. (This is a principle of God's ways in that all our precious things must be given back to God; and then, like it was for Abraham, we receive our "Isaac" back again.)

Whenever David looked on that huge sword, it must have

been a source of great encouragement to his soul. Goliath's sword now back in his hands, would have been a token of God's assurance that his life would indeed be spared. The message of the sword was that the God who preserved his life from the threats of Goliath, will also preserve his life from the dangers of king Saul! Goliath's sword was a pledge and a token of God's love and providential care upon David's life.

It's like God was saying to him, "I saved you in the past and I'll save you now." So, in a time of great distress and upheaval, God graciously gives back to David what he had dedicated to Him when he was a youth!

When we are young and we give to God that which we have; He can always make things come back to us, for our comfort and for our benefit! When young people surrender their lives and their futures to God, He stores those "treasures of the heart" in His *own* tent in Heaven and He can release them back into the world any time He wants. Many people come to the Lord when they're young and He lovingly challenges them to dedicate their lives to His purposes; and it usually involves giving to God everything in their personal "tents."

And so it is for us, in that everything that we consider to be a personal trophy is to be offered back to God, who gave us everything in the first place! This includes our family; our relationships; our careers; our dreams; our future - everything! He is Lord of all or not at all! He will require all the "trophies in our cabinet" because that's what they will remain until we yield them back; and then God can change those trophies into tools! When the prizes of our lives' become God's property, then "the trophy dies and the tool is born." It ceases to be a *memento* of the past and it becomes God's *instrument* for the present day.

God made the trophy of Goliath's sword back into a tool for the Kingdom, and it was placed into the hand of the man whose right it was to have it. Just like this world; one day it will be placed into the hand of the Man whose right it is to have it - the Man, Christ Jesus!

What the contents of this chapter is saying to you, is that God has not forgotten the things you said to Him when you were young. He remembers those words of dedication that you made many years ago, and that you should now make yourself ready to receive the fruit of those decisions. That which you won in Christ in the past by surrendering those trophies to Him, will count again today! They are coming to you because of God's grace upon your life; and like David with the sword of Goliath, there's a sense that you have now proven yourself worthy of them.

Remember, Jesus Christ is Lord of all, not just because God has granted it so, but because He has proved Himself worthy of it; being obedient to God unto death, even the death of a cross! He emptied Himself of all His power and glory to become a man and to become the *Stone* that would slay our great enemy, the Devil.

The Devil was the ultimate Goliath; the ultimate fighting machine, whose sword was death itself! Jesus flung Himself on that "sword of death" so that through death, He might destroy him who had the power of death - that is the Devil. He went to Calvary without a shield and opened His heart for death to strike. He was the "Living Stone" that was flung out of the "sling of God" and it found its mark from Calvary's Cross.

He descended into the lower parts of the earth and there with Death already beaten, He stood over him, drew the "sword of Death" out of its long sheath and with it, slew him! Jesus slew Death with its own sword! The enemy of *every* man was defeated by *one* Man - the Man, Christ Jesus!

Three days later, Jesus walked out of the tomb having the

keys of Death and Hell in His hands. Those trophies are now in His "tent" in Heaven! Hallelujah!

Dear reader, it's time to have some of those things that have been dedicated to God in the past to find a fulfillment today! This message is designed to take the covers off those things which have been hidden in the House of the Lord for many years. This final chapter is a prophetic voice to prepare you to rediscover the "sword of Goliath" in your life. You must reach out and take it when it's offered to you and wage a good warfare with it! Serve the Lord with it and He will continue to deliver you from the paw of the lion; the paw of the bear; and the hand of the giant! There *is* a God in Israel and the battle is the *Lord's!*

Let God turn the trophies of your past into the tools of today!

CLOSING THOUGHTS

In Psalm 103, it tells us that while the Children of Israel saw the acts of the Lord, it was to Moses that He made known His ways.

There was never a man in the Old Testament like Moses, whom the Lord knew face to face. God knew *him* and *he* knew God.

The knowledge that Moses had about God helped him live according to His ways. Sadly, the congregation of the Children of Israel did *not* know the ways of God, and it caused them to grumble and complain about Him - and Moses. There was very little knowledge of God in them and consequently they "strayed in their hearts." They did things that grieved God; even deliberately testing Him at times.

In Psalm 95, it revealed the heart of God pertaining to them when He said, *"For forty years I was grieved with that generation and said 'It is a people who go astray in their hearts, and they do not know My ways.'"* On a later occasion, God spoke through the prophet Isaiah saying, *"My people have gone into captivity because they have no knowledge."* Through yet another prophet, God said, *"My people are destroyed for lack of knowledge."*

As I mentioned in the foreword of this book; Biblical illiteracy is limiting our knowledge and understanding of God. What that means in practical terms is that many Christians are worshiping a God whom they don't really know! And in a fatherless generation, it is of great importance that we at least know our Father in Heaven. Countless Christians become enraged with God when negative things happen in their lives. They simply can't understand what's going on and why certain things have been allowed to take place. They are shocked because they have so little knowledge of Him and His ways. The "doors" of their hearts and minds are closed, because they don't know the Scriptures; neither do they have them expounded to them on a regular basis. The "key" to open up the darkened doors of their minds is the "key of knowledge" - that is the knowledge of God and of Christ as revealed in the Scriptures of Truth. The lawyers of Jesus' day were reprimanded by God for "taking away the key of knowledge" from the people. By so doing, they were blocking the doorway to the Kingdom of Heaven. As a Minister of Christ, my job is to provide access to the door of the Kingdom by giving each one who comes my way the key to get in. That key is the knowledge and the understanding of the Word of God; for it is in Christ and the Scriptures that we have eternal life.

My hope is that having read this book, the reader will have come to know God and His ways a little more. Through the examples that I have given, I trust that the Holy Spirit has given each one the "light of understanding" to what has possibly been some dark times in their lives. Above all, I trust that the contents of this book will cause everyone to want to love and know Him more; and that in their walk with God, their Christian experience will know a greater depth.

'Add to your faith virtue, to virtue knowledge.'

Printed in the United States
By Bookmasters